Just Like Us

Kathy S Aubrey

Finding Friends

in the Word of God

This book is dedicated
to my wonderful husband.

He once asked me this question,
"What three things would you do if money were
no option and you knew you could not fail?"
What you are holding in your hand
is one of my three.

Thanks, Bruce.

Just Like Us

Introduction

Most likely, you have read or studied the ladies you will find in these pages. You may already know their stories. When I studied them closely, I was surprised to learn how similar their lives are to yours and mine, even though they lived so long ago, in an entirely different culture. They had to deal with some of the same issues we do. They had to learn to trust God, just as we have had to do. Sometimes, they chose to disregard God's promptings, and do things their own way. They experienced ups and downs, joys and sorrows, abuses and kindnesses, and other kinds of emotions and treatment. As you read this study, you may also uncover some similarities that are unsettling. These ladies encountered a God who not only knew them and loved them, but also met them in their hour of greatest need.

My prayer is that you might also discover they can be good friends of yours, even if only through the pages of Scripture. After all, they are women just like you.

Eve

Temptation. Even the sound of the word makes my palms sweat. Satan knows our weaknesses, and he goes after them, aggressively. He wants to not only tempt you, but to make you fall, and to fall hard. Eve learned that the hard way.

Creation was finished. God was pleased with His labor. Yes, things were good. Actually, it seemed perfect. God created a man...in His own image. Wow, that is quite awesome. Truly this was Paradise. Take a look at it. Read Genesis 2:1-14, and write down your answers to the following questions. It may seem elementary, yet it will prove to be beneficial.

What did God do after He completed His work? (vv 1-2)

_____

Rest. Don't you just love that word? Allowing yourself time to regain your strength, your health, and your energy is key to being effective in every area of your life. We have the tendency to think we always need to be Wonder Women! Work hard, absolutely, but remember to cease working in order to relax, refresh, and recover. Did you notice in verse 3 that God blessed that day of rest, and called it holy? Jesus invited us to rest as well.

Matthew 11:28-30 *"Come to Me, all you who are weary and burdened, and I will give you* **rest***. Take My yoke upon you and learn from Me, because I am gentle and humble in heart, and you will find* **rest** *for your souls. For My yoke is easy and My burden is light."* HSCB

Use the space below to describe the land before God had finished His work. (vv 4-6)

_____

_____

No shrub, no plant, no rain, no man. Interesting. Now read again the tremendous account of how God made man in verses 7-8.

What did God use to form man?

_____

What did God do to the man to allow him to become a living being?

_____

Can you even imagine this moment in history? God breathed life into him. We could camp out here, but this chapter is about Eve, not Adam, so we press on.

Describe the garden the Lord God planted. (vv 8-10)

_____

_____

_____

I am sure you mentioned the beautiful trees, and the food they must have provided. The colors that radiated from the garden must have been spectacular. I love to be near the water, I imagine the rivers must have been breath taking. And there he was, the man God formed, placed in the garden. Wouldn't you have loved to walk through it? It sounds beautiful.

Do you know of a place that is so gorgeous that it takes your breath away? Describe it.

_____

_____

_____

Read Genesis 2:15. What was God's intent with "the man" and the garden?

_____

_____

In the next three verses, God spoke to the man. God gave him permission, a command, and a statement of intent with a reason. What are they?

Permission to

_____

Command to

_____

Statement of intent to

_____

Reason is because

_____

Clarity is a wonderful thing. Here are some of the questions I find myself asking many times a day (maybe not out loud, but certainly in my head): Why did you do that? What in the world were you thinking? Huh? I don't get it!

Remember this: At this moment, God spoke to the man. The woman had not yet been created. I believe this is a key factor in what we will be reading in a few minutes.

Genesis 2:19-20 tells of all the animals that God created. They were all wonderful, and they still are. Have you been to the zoo lately? Or on a safari, or an aquarium? God is an amazing creator; all His works are incredible. But as wonderful as they were, they could not fill a need in the man's life. According to verse 20, what was that need?

_____

God, again, went into action. He is a need-filling God. What did He do and how? (v 21-22)

_____

_____

_____

I smile every time I read this. God put the man to sleep! Apparently He didn't want his advice on this one. God knew exactly what He wanted, and what the man needed. The man's response in verse 23 could be translated as "Oh, I like it!"

The last two verses in this second chapter describe a marriage. The man leaves his father and mother and bonds with his wife. One flesh, no shame. Wow, that's huge, but again, that is not

8

what this study is about, so on we read.

I have heard it said that the environment is why people sin. You know, the way they were raised, where they grew up, and the people around them. I certainly know that it can be a factor, but here we find Adam and Eve in a perfect environment; sinless, carefree, needs met, no worries, and yet still temptation came and sin was committed. I believe it is more than just the environment; it is the nature of man to sin. No one is perfect. No one is sinless. Satan is banging at our doors to make us believe his lies. He wants us to fall; he wants us to be bound by sin's grip. God wants us free.

Now, we will look closer at Eve. What do we already know about her?

1. She was created by God for Adam.

2. She lived in a perfect environment with Adam...no shame, hurt, envy, bitterness, sorrow, guilt, grief, disease, and on and on it goes.

3. She most likely received God's instruction about the tree of the knowledge of good and evil from Adam, since she had not been created when God told Adam.

In this next passage, Genesis 3:1-5, we read about Eve slipping into sin. So, again, I have to ask... What did she do? And what in the world was she thinking?

Read Genesis 3:1-5 Enter a snake into the garden. I hate snakes. I had a snake in my garden one summer. It gave me the creeps. I saw it first in my garage. I was so startled; my original reaction was a scream. Then I took a shovel, but instead of beating it, I chose to pick it up (with the shovel, of course) and fling it. As it turns out that was a dumb move, since it remained in the vicinity and reared its ugly head several times in the following weeks. No one in my family seemed to be at the same panic level as I, because they had not encountered it. I, however, almost stepped on it twice, and came face to face with it while watering my flowers. After church one Sunday afternoon, I spotted it when I drove in the driveway. I was in a dress, nylons, and heels, but I had had it with this reptile, and today he was going to die. I grabbed an axe from the garage, and started after him. I hurled the axe at him. I missed. He darted away. I followed him, and swung the axe again. Missed again. He slivered away. I raised the axe one more time, missed him again, but this time he coiled himself around the axe. I screamed, of course, and threw the axe. A little boy riding his bicycle stopped and said, "Hey lady, what are you doing?" "I'm trying to kill a snake," I snapped back at him. It was at this moment my neighbors heard the commotion and came to my rescue, much to the snake's demise. We got him. Whew. But I was bothered that the snake had the audacity to think he was welcomed in my garden. Satan is just like that. He takes us by surprise. We cannot anticipate when he will show up. Regardless of how pretty our lives may be, or how perfect and in control we are, we are his targets, and he enjoys slithering into our lives to trick us and coil around us to trap us.

Now let's look closely to what happened in the garden with Eve.

Satan set his trap.

1. <u>He made her question what God said</u>. What did he ask her in Genesis 3:1?

Did God _____ say; you can't eat from any tree in the garden?

2. <u>He made her add to what God had said</u>. (v 3)

...God said, you must not eat it or _____ it, or you will die.

Look back at Genesis 2:17. He said nothing about touching it.

3. <u>Satan contradicts God</u>. (v 4) No you will _____ die, the serpent said to the woman.

He appealed to her "womanly" nature.

1. It was good and delightful.

2. It was desirable for gaining wisdom.

3. It was good enough to share.

Now, what woman could resist that? Don't we like to have our things looking good and delightful? Don't we want our houses to look nice, our clothes to be sharp, our hair to be stylish...Of course, and there is nothing wrong with that, unless it takes us to the place God does not desire us to be.

And what about being in the know? Don't we love to know stuff? Gossip magazines are so popular because we just want to know what is going on with people. The news channels, the newspapers, whatever media form you prefer, it is all because we want to KNOW. Again, nothing wrong there, unless God doesn't want us to know.

Yes, don't we love to share? Spread the wealth, so to speak.

We want everyone to experience what we have. Okay, but be careful, we may just be leading people astray.

Satan does not play fair, this we know. He was too much for Eve to handle on her own. We have all been there. Haven't there been times you have wanted to smack yourself on the forehead, and ask yourself, "Why did I do that?"

Eve gave in, and convinced her honey to do the same. Or maybe he jumped in on his own, we do not know for sure. We do know that the Bible says in Genesis 3:6 that she took the fruit, ate it, and gave some to her husband **who was with her, and he ate it.**

The consequence was just like God had said; they now knew good and evil. Complete this from verse 7:

Then the _____ of them both were opened, they knew they were _____; sewed fig leaves together and made loincloths for themselves.

Embarrassment and shame entered the perfect garden. When they heard God, they hid. We do the same thing, don't we? We think we can hide from His presence.

Read Genesis 3:8-13. What four questions did God ask them?

1. _____

2. _____

3. _____

4. _____

Do you not want to crawl when you have been caught?

Let's press on now and discover what else Eve had to deal with that might be similar to your life and mine.

Genesis 3:16a

_____

Genesis 3:16b

_____

Genesis 3:21

_____

Genesis 4:1-16

_____

Genesis 4:25

_____

Genesis 4:26

_____

There you have it. Many of us have experienced some of the same things: pain in childbirth, struggles with submission, joy of forgiveness and atonement, children that hate each other, a child born even though the heart is breaking, and grandchildren. She endured through it all. Eve is not much different than we are. She suffered great joy and sorrow. She may have been the first to sin, but God had a special blessing for her. We can follow the lineage of her son, Seth, all the way to Jesus.

13

So, my friend, do not despair. God loves you, and has a plan and purpose for your life. Learn to trust Him. Your blessing awaits you.

Close this chapter with prayer.

- Ask God to deliver you from the temptations and traps Satan puts in your way.

- Ask for wisdom and awareness to know when Satan is after you.

- Ask for the strength to walk away and to say no.

- Thank God for His mercy, His forgiveness, and His blessings in your life.

- Thank Him for listening to your cries for help, and for always being there for you.

Sarah

Stress. Life is full of stress. Women have an incredible amount of emotional and mental tension on them. Left unchecked, it can cause havoc on our health and emotions. Many illnesses have a direct line to stress, either causing them, or magnifying them. Doctors tell us that we need to remove the stress from our lives. Okay, but how do you do that? Sounds impossible, but in the pages of Scripture, we can find help from women like Sarah.

It is time to turn a few of your Bible pages until you reach Genesis 11. Read verses 27-32. List all the information you can about Sarai.

_____

_____

_____

Sarai is introduced as Abram's wife. She found herself married to a man who had a definite call from God on his life. One thing for sure, her life would not be dull.

It is unfortunate, but in the pages we will study, we will find her going through much stress and sadness. The first being recorded in chapter 11, verse 30. She was barren. In Bible days, this would have been a huge disappointment, and even considered a curse from God. Imagine the pain that would inflict on a woman's heart. Childlessness is not a curse from God, but it still can cause pain. Perhaps you have dealt with this as well. Or maybe you know someone who has. It could

15

even bring up times of despair over a miscarriage, or death of a child. The pain goes deep, and never completely goes away.

Record your thoughts about the loss of or lack of children.

_____

_____

Yes, the pain runs deep, but we can find comfort in a God who sees, knows, and cares. Glance at Psalm 139. This psalm is a description of how God knows all about us. Not only does He know we are hurting, He knows **why** we are hurting. There are times when that alone brings hope. When it seems like no one else could possibly understand, God does, and He sympathizes with us.

Genesis 12:1-3 records a command and a promise that God gave to Abram. But in the next six verses, we read about the second move Sarai took with her husband. We have already read about her move with Terah, her father-in-law, Abram, and Lot from Ur to Canaan. But as things go sometimes, plans changed along the way and they settled in Haran. It was while in Haran that God spoke to Abram, and off they went again. Where? Not sure. It is like God said, "just go, I will tell you when to stop." I can only imagine how comforting that was. She packed all her stuff, gathered her "people," and off she went. I wonder if she ever thought, "what in the world are we doing? Oh, and why?"

Have you ever moved? What kinds of things are involved in a move that could bring stress? Everyone has a "moving story!"

16

Finish reading the 12th chapter. What happens in the land?

_____

Where do they move this time?

_____

Before they entered Egypt, what request did Abram make of Sarai?

_____

What was it about Sarai that caused him to suggest this? (v 11)

_____

Who would have thought that being beautiful could cause stress???!!!

Reread verse 13. Why did Abram ask her to lie in this way?

_____

This did not go quite like Abram had planned; actually it put his wife in harm's way. I certainly would not have been too happy at this point. How about you?

Scan chapter 13. In verse 1, Abram announced that they were moving again. I can only imagine the conversations that were taking place on the trip, or perhaps, there was no conversation at all. Isn't that just how we respond? When we are mad, someone usually gets an ear full, or the silence is deafening. I am thinking I might have said something like..."Don't you ever do that to me again. You got that?"

17

Throughout this chapter, Lot is referred to quite often. This study is not about him, nor his relationship with Abram, but let's just say, this particular family member was adding more stress to an already tense situation. He would have sent me right over the edge!

Let's fast forward to Genesis 16:1-5.

Verse one repeats an issue with Sarai. What is it?

_____

Same verse, who is Hagar, and where did she use to live?

_____

Egypt...remember that Egypt wasn't too kind to Sarai. Bad memories and now she had a slave that she gained while she was there. In hindsight, probably not such a good idea. We will be looking closer at Hagar, next, so let's still focus on Sarai.

Sarai is stressed about not having children. She came up with this really bad plan to have her slave, Hagar, bear children for her. Abram agreed. Don't even get me started with this one. I am no genius, but even I can see trouble on the horizon with this plan. Apparently, she was desperate to have children, and this seemed to be the only way.

What happened after Hagar became pregnant with Abram's child?

with Hagar in verse 4: _____

with Sarai in verse 5 _____

18

Verse 6:

with Abram _____

with Sarai _____

with Hagar _____

Just for fun, imagine you have been asked to counsel Abram, Sarai, and Hagar. What would you have said to them?

_____

_____

Let's wrap up our look at Sarai by reading just three more brief passages. We will begin to see the turn-around for Sarai. She finally finds peace and her stress levels decrease.

Read Genesis 17:15-16.

Apparently the first change had to come from Abraham. God had already changed his name (v 5). In this passage, God told Abraham to not call her Sarai any more. What does He tell him to call her?

_____

What does He also tell Abraham He is going to do for her?

_____

Sarah means princess. God promised to bless her, give her a son, and produce nations through her. Could it be that now she would be treated like a princess, so she would feel like a princess, and she would start acting like a princess?

It makes such a huge difference in self-esteem. It is crucial to know who God says you are. It is essential to know that He has a plan and a purpose for your life.

How do you see yourself?

_____

How does God see you?

_____

Read Jeremiah 29:11. You can claim that verse as your own.

Genesis 18:11-15: Sarah heard God's promise to both of them with her own ears. Have you heard God speak to you through His Word? Describe it below.

_____

_____

Now read Genesis 21:1-2.   *The Lord came to Sarah as He had said......* oh how I love that.

and the Lord did for Sarah as He had promised.... oooh, love that too.

Are you still waiting for God to speak to you, and to fulfill His promise? Write below that promise, than ask once more for God to answer that prayer, and to give you grace as you wait for Him.

20

Hagar

Betrayal. In our life, we will experience some sort of betrayal. It hurts when those we trust and love turn on us with their actions or by their words. It leaves our thoughts in turmoil and our hearts in knots. How can we possibly trust again? The answer can be found in the next look at a woman just like us.

We already had a quick glance at Hagar. We know she was Sarai's Egyptian maidservant. With that being her role, she was at Sarai's every beck and call, obligated to her every wish and command. We also know that she became a maternity surrogate for Sarai, but let's read it again, focusing this time on Hagar. Read Genesis 16:1-6.

Did Hagar have any say in this plan of Sarai's? _____

Why or why not?

_____

Have you ever been in a situation that changed everything for you, yet you had no say in the decision? If so, what was it, and how did it affect you?

_____

_____

Sarai obviously made this decision in panic mode. When decisions are made under those circumstances, generally people get hurt.

According to verse 4, what happened with Hagar after she

learned she was pregnant?

_____

Why do you think that happened?

_____

_____

In verse 5, on whom did Sarai place the blame? _____

How did Abraham react to this blame? (v 6)

_____

_____

Hagar was in a lose-lose situation. Sarai turned on her, and Abram turned on her. Betrayal does a number on an individual. Yes, Hagar looked down on Sarai, She despised her. That is definitely harsh. Remember though, the gal was pregnant. There are physiological and emotional changes that take place in the woman's body during pregnancy. She most likely felt unwanted, used, abused, and betrayed. That's a really harmful combination. Now, top that with Abram giving Sarai permission to do whatever she wanted to do with Hagar. Oh, boy.

What did Sarai do to Hagar? (v 6)

_____

How did Hagar respond this time?

_____

Yes, she ran away. Can you blame her? Jot down some ways you have reacted in the past to being mistreated and betrayed?

_____

_____

_____

_____

Read Genesis 16:7-16

Who found Hagar? _____

What did He ask her?

_____

Hagar ran away, but the Angel of the Lord found her. Isn't that just like God? There is not a place we can run that He will not find us. Did you notice that He even called her by her name? I love that. God knows your name too. If you are at a place in your life where you are "running away," you might as well slow down. He is running with you. In fact, listen carefully, and you will hear Him call your name, and ask you the same questions. Where have you come from? Where are you going?

_____

_____

_____

In verse 9, the Angel gave specific instructions to Hagar. What were they?

_____

_____

_____

_____

Go back. As hard as it may be, there are times you just have to go back to where your life started to fall apart. The healing begins at the spot that the hurt began. I do not always understand how that works, but I know it does. Can you think of a time in your life that it worked that way?

Submit. Not a popular word, especially in this context, because Hagar was told to submit to her mistreatment. Yikes. That's harsh. But even when it doesn't seem clear, nor even make sense, you must do the right thing...do what God says. Can you think of a time when it was hard, and you wanted to fight it, but you did the right thing, and God blessed it? Record it below.

_____

_____

Did you notice that there was also a promise to Hagar that God would multiply her? Sure, the words she heard that day by the water were not rosy, but she did have an encounter with the Almighty God. In fact, what name did she give the LORD? (v 13) _____

Have you had an encounter with God that was yours alone, and you too could call Him The God Who Sees? Describe it.

_____

_____

_____

Turn the pages in your Bible to Genesis 21:8-21. Here we read of another meeting between Hagar and God. At this time, Ishmael had already been born, in fact, when Sarah gave birth to the son she was promised, Ishmael was a teenager.

In verses 8-9, what does Sarah observe Ishmael doing?

_____

Knowing all that had happened before, why do you suppose this made her so angry?

_____

Sarah demanded a very difficult thing of Abraham. It is obvious things are still not good between Hagar and Sarah. This particular aggravation was of Ishmael's doing, not Hagar, yet she received the brunt of Sarah's ire.

What was Abraham's reaction? (vv 11-14)

_____

_____

Abraham was grieved. Ishmael was his son. He would always

be, regardless of whether he had done right or wrong. Because we know the end of the story, we know what God says to him is true. How difficult do you think God's word of comfort would have been to believe? (v12)

_____

_____

_____

Abraham sent the two of them away. This must have seemed familiar to Hagar, but this time she left with her son. They were in the wilderness, and Hagar prepared for them to die.

Hagar distanced herself from her boy (v16). Why?

_____

Have you ever experienced pain and grief so heavy, that you had to try to get away from it? Notice too, that her grief was so strong, she too wept loudly. There is nothing wrong with crying, sobbing, or wailing. It does not change the situation, nor does it make one feel better, but it releases the emotion that is within your heart. And of course, we know Who sees and understands the heart.

Record who heard the boy? (v17)

_____

From where?

_____

Once again, in her pit of despair, betrayal, grief, and sorrow, she heard God call her name. "What's wrong, Hagar?" I imagine she remembered that voice, and perhaps new hope filled her heart. What were His instructions this time?

_____

_____

Those same instructions may be ours too. Think about it.

Don't be afraid. Does anything have you worried or afraid?

God has heard the cry... Have you wondered if God has heard your cry for help?

Get up. Is He telling you to get up, move on, and deal with it?

Help the boy, sustain him. Is there a task you have been asked to do for someone else, or for yourself?

Look what happened next for Hagar. (v 19) God opened her eyes, and there before her was the very answer for her and her dying son. It was water for Hagar.

What is it for you? What does God want to show you, if you will only open your eyes? If you know, write it down.

No, Hagar's life was not perfect after that, far from it. Neither will yours be. But, you too can find refuge, life, and hope in the God Who Sees.

Lot's Wife

Worldliness = of or concerned with material values or ordinary life rather than a spiritual existence. The definition alone sends out a warning siren, does it not? Keep the verse written below in mind as we study Lot's Wife.

> *Therefore, put to death whatever in you is worldly:*
> *sexual immorality, impurity, lust, evil desire,*
> *and greed, which is idolatry.*
> Colossians 3:5

In Luke 17:32, Jesus told his disciples to "remember Lot's wife." Why? What was it about her that Jesus would specifically pull her out of Scripture, and admonish his disciples, and us, to remember her? What is He saying to us?

Let's start first by the context of this verse. Read Luke 17:20-36. What is the topic of communication?

_____

Jesus compares these days to two sets of "days". What are they?

_____

_____

What was going on during these days?

_____

28

What about now? Are the days in which we are living similar to the days described in these verses? They certainly are. So Jesus' instructions apply to us today. Remember Lot's Wife.

Remember is such a great word. It's a word of awareness of something or someone in the past (Remember the Alamo!)

- It's a word to remind us of something that must be done (Remember to take out the trash).

- It's a word used to emphasize something (Remember to keep it a secret).

- It's word used for protection (Remember to look both ways before crossing the street).

- It's a word used for our health (Remember to take your vitamins).

And on and on it goes. So there is a very good reason, Jesus told us to remember. Let's find out why.

The wife of Lot; we do not know her name, but she is someone with whom we need to get acquainted. Her husband had quite a reputation as well. Learning about him can help shed light on who she was.

Lot's relatives go all the back to Noah. Noah had three sons, Ham Shem, and Japheth. His son, Shem, is the lineage that leads to Terah. Terah was the father of Abram, Nahor, and Haran. Haran fathered Lot, which makes him Abram's nephew. (Genesis 11:10-32)

There certainly was a lot of drama surrounding this family. In Genesis chapter 12 we read about God's call on Abram's life and his instructions to leave the land of his relatives. In verses 4-5, we discovered that Abram obeyed, but took Lot with him.

In verse 5 of the next chapter, we learned that Lot followed Abram wherever he went. Lot became a rich man. He had flocks, herds, tents, livestock, and herdsmen. His possessions were many. There was quarreling between his men and Abram's men. It became apparent that separation was needed. Lot was allowed to choose which land he would settle. If he chose to go one way, then Abram would take the other way. Lot chose the best land.

Lot's wife had been dragged to several different locations. She most likely had witnessed the bickering and tension between Lot's "stuff" and Abram's. She had gained much wealth, and observed when her husband selfishly chose the well-watered, plush land, while the elderly uncle was given the less desirable land. I am not suggesting that she was corrupted by her husband or his business dealings, but I am wondering about the influence their life-style had made on her.

Look carefully now at Genesis 13:12-13. Where was Lot living? _____

Where had he set up his tent? _____

Describe the men of Sodom.

_____

Genesis 14 records an event when Lot had to be rescued by Abram, as he had been taken prisoner during a war. Notice where Lot was. Genesis 14:12

He was _____
in Sodom.

Turn a few pages, and read Genesis 19:1. Where was Lot sitting? _____

The fact that he was sitting at the gate suggests that he now held some kind of" governmental" office. To me this is a troubling progression: From a tent NEAR Sodom, to living IN Sodom, to "GOVERNING" Sodom.

It is a dangerous thing to toy with sin. At times we get just as close as we can and believe we are still safe. Satan loves it when we are think we are safe. But, when we get that close, we become bigger targets and the temptations are greater and harder to resist. Sodom lured Lot and his wife into its nasty grip, so much so, the city, and its evil, became home to them. They were comfortable there.

What was so bad about Sodom, anyway? Genesis 18:16 – 19:29 tells its ugly story. God decided He had had about all He could take. He told Abraham of His plan to destroy it.

Genesis 18:20 How was their sin described?

_____

According to Genesis 19:1-9, what kind of behavior took place openly in Sodom?

_____

Verse 8 is the telltale description of the kind of parents Lot and his wife were. What did Lot offer the men of Sodom?

_____

Doesn't that make you sick to your stomach? All over the world women are exploited, mistreated, and abused. I am so grateful for the love God has for women and girls. Though we are surrounded by perversion, pornography, seduction, and every other kind of hatred toward women, God pursues us and holds us in high esteem. We captivate him. Believe it and teach it to the girls and women in your life.

Who assisted Lot out of this awful situation?

_____

Lot tried, on his own, to fight off the evil. The angel reached down, grabbed him (*by the seat of his pants*, my words, not God's), and brought him into the house.

Then at the beginning of the destruction of Sodom and Gomorrah, Lot hesitated in leaving. Who assisted him this time? _____

The angels of God again had to intervene. They grabbed Lot's hand, his wife's hand, and their daughters' hands and dragged them to the outside of the city. Even though they knew the city would be destroyed, they would not leave on their own. Unbelievable.

They stopped and settled in Zoar. What happened there?

_____

Lot and his family reached Zoar. The sulfur fell and burned up the cities of Sodom and Gomorrah, and all their inhabitants. Then it happened.... Lot's wife looked back. She became a pillar of salt. People may ask, "seriously?" The answer is yes. The Bible says it ... it is true.

Lot, Lot's wife, and their two daughters had been drastically influenced by the evil in Sodom. You can read about another detestable act from this family, specifically the daughters in Genesis 19:30-33. My mind keeps screaming three questions. Why? What were they thinking? What went wrong?

Obviously Lot and the girls had their own issues, but our focus now is Lot's wife. Why did she look back?

I do not think she looked back with the intent to watch the tragedy. I think she looked back with sadness because she had been forced to leave. The place she loved was being destroyed.

I believe that Lot's wife had chains of worldliness. The habits and relationships that developed from her immoral lifestyle became chains around her heart. God was reaching out for her over and over, but she resisted and ignored His help. Her heart was too attached. The world's grip was too tight. She did not even realize the freedom God was offering to her.

Now, let's get real. Are there times in your life that you know God tried to save you from a bad situation, yet you resisted his help, or ignored it? If so, what did you learn from that experience?

Do you have any unhealthy attachments, either with people or with things or habits? Are you willing to rid yourself of them WITH God's help?

Do you love the things of the world more than the things of God? Oh, I pray we will learn to listen to the voice of God and heed His instructions. Just like God's desire was for Lot's wife to be rescued, He desires for us to be free as well. I pray that we will be strong enough to turn our backs on the things that turn us away from God.

Rebekah

Deception. Lies. Schemes. Such ugly words. Uglier still when they become a way of life. Even a beautiful lady with great potential can be lured away by the enemy. He is a tough opponent. He can twist our thinking, so we believe that the wrong way is the right way. Look out, he works slowly and subtly.

When we first meet Rebekah, we immediately fall in love with her. Abraham wanted the perfect wife for his son, Isaac. He gave one of his servants the task to go find her. Not an easy task, for sure. I mean, we are talking "Isaac" here. Genesis 24 tells the account. In verses 12-14, the servant asked for God's help. He knew what was on the line. He needed this to go well. Verse 15 is one of my favorites in this passage. It is like a great romance. Read the chapter from the start, but then answer the questions below about verses 15-27.

Who appeared before he had finished praying?

_____

(Don't you love it when the answer to your prayer starts happening even before you are finished asking God?)

Who is she?

_____

What is she carrying on her shoulder?

_____

Aha!... he must have thought! I asked for a gal, who needed water, and she has a jug, and she is walking my way.

34

You know what, I believe it is fine to come to God with a list. When you know what you want, some things are automatically weeded-out!

Describe Rebekah from verse 16.

_____

_____

_____

Rebekah was beautiful. She hadn't known a man intimately (good for her). The romance was coming together nicely. As we read on, we discover it all happened just like Abraham's servant requested. In fact, what did he do in verse 26-27?

_____

How sweet is verse 28? Rebekah ran to tell her family the news. I have tried to picture in my mind what that would have been like. I remember telling my family members that I was in love and I was going to get married. The thought of it makes me smile with the remembered anticipation. I wanted to laugh, scream, and cry all at the same time. I think Rebekah may have had some of the same thoughts.

As the story was retold to Rebekah's family, Laban and Bethuel, realized this was from the Lord, and agreed to let Rebekah return to Abraham with their daughter. Read the account of when Rebekah and Isaac met (verses 52-67). It is truly a wonderful love story. She was what Isaac needed. He was also what she needed.

Rebekah had her weaknesses. We all do. Rebekah allowed her

insecurity to overshadow her good qualities.

Read Genesis 25:19-28. What is the condition she shared with her mother-in-law?

_____

When did she conceive?

_____

What kind of pregnancy did she experience?

_____

_____

What question did she ask? (v 22)

_____

Have you ever asked that same question concerning something you were facing? Yes, me too.

Rebekah inquired of God. That's good thinking. Ask the One who knows all things. He does have an answer. We will not always know the answer this side of Heaven, but that is when we need to trust in the God who created us and loves us.

Let me make a quick observation for us here that we will refer back to later. Isaac was 40 when he and Rebekah were married. He was 60 when the twins were born.

Now let's take a look at the boys. Read verses 27-34 from chapter 25. Describe the boys.

36

Esau

_____

_____

Jacob

_____

_____

Favoritism played a major role in the chaos to come. Who favored whom?

Isaac favored _____ because

_____

Rebekah favored _____

Any thoughts why?

_____

_____

Read ahead to Genesis 26:34-35. What made Rebekah bitter?

_____

Genesis 27 is the sad account of the tension and rivalry between Jacob and Easu. It was made worse by the role that Rebekah played. She was intent on <u>her</u> favorite receiving the blessing from his father; she plotted the entire deception. Why? How did she get to this place?

Her mistakes were many. Let's list some of them. Beware; you may see that we are not too far from where she was. The faces in our lives may be different, and the names may be different, but the choices may be all too familiar.

v 5	eavesdropping
vv 8-17	scheming against authority
v 18	deceiving her husband, and involving her son in the lie
v 34	caused great agony for her son
v 41	stirred more anger between brothers where hatred already existed

Now let's go back to the ages of Isaac. We know Esau was 40 when he was married (Genesis 26:34), and that the birthright occasion took place after that. Since Isaac was 60 when the boys were born, that makes him at least 100 at this point. What would possess a woman to deceive her husband of that age? Jacob was 40. Don't you think that is too old to play such a trick on your father and your brother? Don't you think they both should have known better? There is no age-limit to sin. God help us.

Record some of your thoughts.

_____

_____

When Rebekah learned how angry Esau was, even knowing the pain her plot caused everyone, she still tried to control the circumstances. In the process of trying to protect Jacob from his brother, she sent him away, never to see him again. Her attempt at promoting her favored son, brought grief to her own heart, not to mention the family dynamics that remained.

Can you think of a time when you took matters into your own hands, and the outcome was not a good one?

_____

_____

Were you ever able to make it right? If not, and if there is still time, what do you think the Lord is telling you to do?

Rachel and Leah

Jealousy. There are few issues that create more havoc and destruction than jealousy. This culprit lingers everywhere. We can get jealous over things, people, places, and positions. It can wreck relationships. Hopes and dreams can be zapped. It creeps up on us inconspicuously. Jealousy certainly stirred up trouble between Rachel and Leah.

Rachel and Leah were sisters. They should have been friends, but Rachel was jealous of Leah, and Leah was jealous of Rachel, for different reasons, but the "game" was on between them. They teach us the importance of finding our worth and our identity in God, not by looking in the mirror and critiquing ourselves, nor by comparing ourselves to others.

Genesis 29 starts out like another romance story. The first time Jacob sees Rachel is what good chick-flicks are all about. There are a few sirens that start to sound in my head as I read this account. Let's take a look.

Read the first 12 verses of chapter 29.

How is the setting similar to that of Abraham's servant looking for Isaac's wife?

_____

Who was seen walking toward Jacob?

_____

Whose daughter is she? _____

Whose brother is Laban? _____

Not sure about you, but that makes me a little nervous. Rebekah did not always have the best judgment...I have to think, is it a family trait??!!

I laugh at verse 11. What did Jacob do after he kissed Rachel? _____ Is that a siren I hear in your head too?

What did Rachel do next according to verse 12?

_____

She ran to tell daddy... remember how Rebekah ran home after she met Abraham's servant? Let's read on...Genesis 29:16-18

Describe the sisters:

Rachel _____

_____

Leah _____

_____

Which sister captured Jacob's attention? _____

What was the agreement between Jacob and Laban? (vv 18-20)

_____

_____

In verse 21, Jacob is ready to take his bride. The celebration took place. But Laban, like his sister, schemed to trick Jacob. What was it? (vv 23-29)

_____

_____

_____

So like it or not, Jacob had both Rachel and Leah as wives, as well as Zilpah (Leah's) and Bilhah (Rachel's) as maidservants to the girls. As they say at the Olympics, "let the games begin!"

Read Genesis 29:30. List one problem between the girls.

_____

You most likely wrote something like this, Jacob loved Rachel more than Leah.

Find another problem between the girls: Genesis 29:31-35

_____

Leah was having children and Rachel was barren. Did you pick up the thought in Leah's mind? She believed that by bearing children, she would gain the love of her husband. Can you imagine how Leah must have hurt? She lacked her sister's beauty and her husband's love. My guess her self-worth and self-esteem was destroyed.

Do you or someone you know struggle with self worth or self-respect. Describe what that is like, how is it manifested?

42

Leah stopped having children after she gave birth to Judah. He was from this lineage that Jesus was born. (See Matthew 1). What changed in Leah's focus and heart after this birth? (v 35)

———————————————————————————

What a difference our focus makes. It is a choice---choose to praise the Lord. It may not change our circumstances, but it does change our thoughts and our hearts. It also will help us to make wiser decisions. But it is hard work to stay there. Satan battles for our mind, daily.

Now, on to Rachel. Let's look to see how she was dealing with all the babies.

Genesis 30:1 states a third problem between the sisters. What is it?

———————————————————————————

Rachel envied Leah. Jealousy, the green-eyed monster.

Read Genesis 30:2-8. My head spins when I read this. Rachel's jealousy and competition with her sister created a mess. Her desire for children distorted her thinking, and made her husband angry. Yet, don't you agree that Jacob could have said no at some point? Reading further in the chapter, Leah sent her maidservant to Jacob too, and things kept getting crazier. Before God opened Rachel's womb, (v 22-24), Jacob had ten sons. I again have to laugh when I read verse 26. Jacob said to Laban ..."you know how hard I have worked for you." Ha-ha, I guess he had! The 2 wives, the 2 slave girls, all the boys, and Laban! He was worn out for sure.

Has jealousy ever created a problem in any of your relationships?

Women are prone to compete, and/or to make ourselves the forever victim. When it leads us to sin, it seems we quickly respond with more sin. May God give us the grace and wisdom to see ourselves as He sees us, and to live above the fray. He loves us, has a plan and a purpose for us. Dwell there, my friend, dwell there.

Tamar

Daughter-in-law of Judah

Deceit: action or practice of misleading someone by concealing or misrepresenting the truth

So rid yourselves of all wickedness, all deceit,
hypocrisy, envy, and all slander.
2 Peter 2:1

No question about it, life can throw mud at you. It is unfortunate, but some of the greatest sorrows that come our way, are delivered from family members. Even Jesus' family tree grew some blemished branches.

Read Matthew 1:3. Tamar is listed in the genealogy of Jesus. Who are the people that will be important for us to know?

The father: _____

The sons: _____

and_____

Which son has the direct lineage? _____

Tamar's story is painful. She suffered loss, pain, and much humiliation. Before we read about her, it is necessary for us to understand a levirate marriage law.

Read Deuteronomy 25:5-6.

The purpose of this Hebrew law was to carry on the family line in honor of the dead man's name and inheritance. So, if a man died, the man's brother married his wife in order to bear children. It would also insure land distribution. When the widow would bear her firstborn son, the child would legally be the dead man's son and would inherit the dead man's property. This law builds the groundwork for the biography of Tamar.

Read Genesis 38:1-6. Time to study the family tree. Judah is one of the twelve sons of Jacob.

Who is Judah's wife? _____

What are the names of their three boys?

_____, _____, _____

Where was the third child born? _____

Interesting note here is that the Hebrew root of this name/word is the same root word that means deception, a theme we see throughout this story.

Which son married Tamar? _____

In the remaining verses of this chapter, we learn the dismal story of Tamar. Read vv 7-10.

Describe Er. _____

What happened to him? _____

Did you gasp when you read that? Me too. It bothered me, but it is what it is. He was evil, God was not pleased with it, and He ended Er's life. God did a similar thing with the evil people in Noah's day by sending the flood.   Sodom and Gomorrah were destroyed by sulphur and fire.   God takes "evil" seriously.

By levirate law, brother Onan took Tamar.   This man used Tamar for sexual pleasure and had no intention of giving her an offspring.   God considered what Onan had done evil as well. Now two brothers are gone.

Read verse 11. Who was next? _____

Judah twisted the law just a bit.   Tamar should have gone to live in his household, since he was the father of Er.   Instead, he told her to stay in her own father's house until his last little boy grew up.   Sounds fine, but again, deception reared its ugly head.   He never intended to give Shelah to Tamar.   Why?

_____

_____

Verse 12 … who was next to die? _____

Judah had mourned, and the verse stated he was on his way to Timnah to the sheepshearers.   Tamar had her own plan of deception.   Read vv 13-30.

The story played out like a soap opera, perhaps even real life for some.   What is obvious is hurt, anger, and pain, left unattended makes people do some outrageous things.   Hurt people hurt people.   But it is not unusual to see sex used as a weapon to get revenge, to get what you want, or to get even.

What do you believe was Tamar's motive in this scheme?

_____

She was smooth, no doubt. She had her mind set, and she knew how to pull this off. Judah was most likely vulnerable, for two reasons. He had deceived Tamar, so he was a prime candidate for being deceived. He was lonely and hungry for a woman's attention ... remember, he had just lost his wife.

Women were considered a lower class of people. They were worthy only if they could bear children, especially a son to carry on the family line. Tamar wanted a child to honor her husband. Tamar had more issues. She had lost her spouse, been misused by her brothers-in-law, humiliated, and lied to, so frankly, she was mad. As is so often the case, it doesn't make it right, but it is understandable.

For what did she ask in lieu of payment for her "services?" vv 17-20 _____

What was Judah going to pay her? _____

(A goat... Oh, for crying out loud!)

Another turn of events occurred in vv 21-23, what was it?

_____

_____

Judah assumed Tamar was a harlot, never did he believe for a moment that she was his daughter-in-law. When he learned that no shrine prostitutes "worked" in the place, he shrugged it off and allowed his cord, seal, and staff to remain with the girl. In today's society, the equivalent possession would be a credit cards, a driver's license, or even a social security card. They were uniquely Judah's, no doubts or confusion.

48

Reread verse 23. According to this verse, what was Judah's reasoning to forget about getting his pledge back?

_____

_____

Before we move on, it is best we understand this fact: cult or shrine prostitutes were commonplace in this pagan culture. A private prostitute however was punished when caught.

My guess is Judah never expected a pregnancy to result, and thought this sin of his would simply disappear over time.

He had heard that Tamar was pregnant and most likely thought it was a result of harlot activity. Judah was angry, and requested her death; then his seal, cord, and staff were sent to him by Tamar. Imagine his surprise. He could not deny that they were his.

Verse 26 reveals Judah's recognition of his own wrongdoing toward Tamar. What was it?

_____

_____

_____

Another detail is given about their relationship, what was it?

_____

_____

From that point on, Judah respected Tamar and kept their relationship pure.

Tamar gave birth to twins. What were their names?

_____ and _____

Which child became a direct line to Jesus? _____

Tamar was desperate, not wicked. The men in her life had betrayed and failed her. Nevertheless, her actions were indeed sinful and in violation of God's laws.

God can make all things work together for good. I love that about Him. No one is too good that they do not need Him, and no one is so bad that they cannot find Him.

We are drawn to deceitfulness, but it does not have to keep us bound. If this is an area where you are weak, beg God to break away those chains of deceit and set you free. Ask Him to heal your hurting heart, and tell Him you desire to be walking in truth.

Rise above your pain, my friends, let it go.

Potiphar's Wife

Potiphar's wife … this gal had it all. Her husband had a high-ranking position. She was spoiled by her surroundings and her husband. She lived in a gorgeous home and was wealthy. Everything she had was in abundance. Her extravagant life did not make her who she was, it merely revealed who she was.

Begin reading her story in Genesis 39: 1- 6

Let's develop the setting. Fill in the details.

Joseph has been taken to _____(country)

Potiphar is an officer of _____and

the _____ of the guard.

Joseph was _bought_ by _____.

Joseph was a unique man. Why? The Bible says,

The Lord _____ _____ Joseph.

He (Joseph) became a _____ man.

The Lord _____ he did

_____.

Joseph found _____ in his master's sight.

This passage goes on to state that the Egyptian house was blessed, and God's blessing was on all that Potiphar owned because of Joseph. Potiphar worried about nothing.

That's amazing. Joseph was an upright man and others were blessed because of him. If you glance back at where Joseph had come, and what he had endured, it is truly a testimony of God's faithfulness and Joseph's faith that he was still standing tall on his own feet. Most of us would be in a pit somewhere, still wondering what happened, and giving up on life. I guess it is true, what doesn't kill you only makes you stronger.

Read on; verses 7-11. Again let's focus on the facts first.

Who had an uncontrollable attraction to Joseph?

_____

What did she want from him?

_____

What was the reasoning behind Joseph's refusal?

_____

_____

_____

This evil, this sin, would be against whom? _____

How often did her request occur?

_____

Most likely Potiphar's wife was empty, or perhaps she was nursing an insatiable appetite. Either case is dangerous. She was not being filled with what she had, or it just wasn't enough for her any more. She was not a believer, so God was not on her radar. She apparently was searching for something to fill that void, and when her eyes caught Joseph, she would not resist. No doubt there was a physical attraction. The Bible says Joseph was handsome and well built. What she felt, however, was not love, but lust.

Lust leads to misery. Potiphar's wife was accustomed to getting what she wanted, and she wanted Joseph. But he turned her down. She became pushy and more seductive. She went after him day after day.

Women can become aggressive in areas of their weaknesses. We must be very cautious of where we allow our thoughts and our behavior to roam. There are so many ways to wander from the godly, moral, and healthy lives God has for us. (Television, internet, movies, magazines, books, stores) Pornography, adultery, fornication, flirting, immorality, it all knocks at your door, day after day, begging for your attention and involvement. Guard your hearts, ladies. Temptations are real and strong. Be prepared to fight. Prepare for your battle before it begins. Determine to stand strong, just like Joseph.

For those of you who are married, or will soon be, stand in the gap for your husbands by praying for their protection against unwanted attention from women. A godly man is an attraction. Satan desires to take out godly marriages, and ruin reputations. He is waiting, chain in hand, to trap you and your husband and make you stumble.

One more "soapbox" before we get back to Potophar's house. Notice again what Joseph called her proposition. Sin. Sin against God. Have you notice that in today's society we have renamed what God has called sin? We have given in to the futile attempt at making our sin not seem so bad.

Can you think of examples? _____

_____

_____

_____

Now back to the house. Read verses 11-20. We will take it verse by verse.

v. 11   Joseph was working, even when no one else was there. Don't you just love a faithful employee? He didn't just work while he was being watched, or while the boss was in the house. Joseph was a faithful worker.

v. 12   Potiphar's wife grabbed him. She grabbed him in such a way, that Joseph slipped out of his garment and ran outside. Good for him. I say, run Joseph, run. What a powerful lesson for us. He did not stay and try to reason with her again. Something about what she did this time felt different to him. Joseph knew he had to get out of there. So again I say to you, my friend, when Satan brings that temptation and it "grabs" you...run, baby, run! Do not try to reason your way out, just RUN! Anyone ever stay when they should have run? Painful memories, I am sure of it. Wouldn't you like an undo/redo button?

v. 13   *When she realized* ... I have to admit, I smile a little at this verse. It is like she was shocked momentarily and had to get her wits about her again. Joseph ran from her like a bunny running from a fox! How dare he? Who does he think he is? Does he have any idea who he just turned down? She had been deprived of what she really wanted, rejected. I think she was stunned that he did not want her and that she did not get her way. She was angry.

v. 14-18   Now the revenge and "you will pay' game began. She lied about what happened. No big surprise there! She was well aware of how angry Potiphar would be at Joseph if he believed her lies. She was right about that.

vv. 19-20   Joseph's punishment, even though he was innocent and above the reproach, was severe.

Potiphar's wife twisted the truth. She knew she was wrong, but her warped ego could not tolerate the humiliation she was feeling. So again she lashed out at Joseph, this time involving her husband, on whom she was ready to cheat. She did not love him either. Her love was all tied up in her own desires. She used her position to bring Joseph to ruin. She made her husband believe a lie about a trusted friend and worker. Potiphar did not even investigate the allegation. He believed his wife, how ironic. She was unfaithful and vindictive due to a lust that had a chain around her heart.

Potiphar's wife showed no sorrow, asked no forgiveness, nor ever attempted to right her wrong. In fact she is not mentioned again in Scripture.

Joseph's life would not have included prison bars, if she would have chosen to let God break her chains of lust and free her from the void that she had within her heart. No, she never experienced the freedom, but she teaches us the importance of allowing God to fill our void and emptiness with His grace and His peace.

Jochebed

We are now going to advance our study to the book of Exodus. The main character in this book is Moses. He will not be the focus of this chapter, however he plays a role in the analysis of Jochebed, his mother. Read Exodus 1 to get a feel for the historical background, then answer the questions below.

Why were the Israelites living in Egypt?

_____

_____

Why was the Egyptian king threatened by the number of Israelites now living in Egypt?

_____

_____

What was the plan to keep the Israelites "controlled?"

_____

When his Plan A did not work, what was his Plan B?

_____

Why did this plan not work?

_____

_____

What was Pharaoh's Plan C?

_____

_____

Now that we are familiar with the back-story, let's read on to the next chapter. Exodus 2:1-4.

For whatever reason, the names of the "man from the family of Levi" and the "Levite woman" are not mentioned here. However, turn to Exodus 6:20 and Numbers 26:59. What are their names?

The man from the family of Levi

_____

The Levite woman

_____

Their two boys _____

and _____

Their daughter _____

Jochebed lived in bondage in Egypt. She became pregnant and gave birth to a son. The Bible states that the baby was beautiful. She hid him for three months, but the fact that he survived his birth was miraculous since the midwives were instructed to kill all baby boys when they were born. Then there was the evil command that if any male infants survived they would be thrown into the Nile.

I cannot fathom such hatred. The ancient pharaohs hated Yahweh, and likewise they hated the Israelites. I am amazed at the keen faith expressed by this woman whose name means Yahweh's Glory. As a mother, her heart must have been in such fear at the thought of the destruction of her beautiful baby boy. Could she hide him? How could she keep him quiet, so the Egyptian taskmasters would not hear nor see him? Would God protect her family? Would He truly give her this boy, only to have him killed? Was she brave enough to carry out her plan? What would happen to her son?

Fear can paralyze us. No matter the magnitude of the situation, fear stops us in our tracks, and unless it is dealt with, we are unable to think rationally or live effectively. Fear can take on many forms as well. It can produce danger, threat, anxiety or panic.

Even though fear is a common emotion with us, the things we fear can be so very different. What things right now have your heart gripped with fear?

_____

_____

_____

Until we lay all those fears at the Lord's feet, they will be like chains we drag with us everywhere we go. The weight gets so heavy. Can't we trust God? Don't we know He is able to take our fears? Tell Him what they are. Tell Him how scared and fearful you are. Ask Him to have His will in all of the situations that are causing you to worry and fret. Then ask Him for His help to allow your heart to experience peace, His peace in the middle of your storm. Read His Word, using a concordance to search for verses about fear; claim them, and remind God of what He has promised. Then believe Him. He can do what He says He can do.

Jochebed must have believed that God's power was stronger than her enemy's. She proceeded with strength in the midst of her fear. According to verse 2 what did she do and for how long?

_____

Three months. The days of those months must have been bathed in prayer, as well as developing a plan to protect her baby. What was her plan?

_____

_____

This lady amazes me. She made a basket, a hand made ark, if you will, big enough for her three-month-old child. What three ingredients do she use?

_____, _____

and _____

Papyrus was abundant in Egypt. It is a plant that is found next to water. It grows 10-20 feet tall. Strips of it were used to form a sheet, weaving the strips both horizontally and vertically. It was then pressed, dried, and rubbed smooth. It became the paper on which ancient documents were written. It is possible that Jochebed followed similar steps to weave the basket that would house her little child.

Asphalt was a mixture of sand, gravel and clay.

Pitch, also called bitumen, was a natural black tarlike mixture.

Can you picture this desperate mother; building this little home, praying it will be the protection needed for her son? As she wove the papyrus strips, molding them into a boat-like shape, covering it with the tarlike substance that would keep out the water, and hold the smell of human inside the basket, can't you imagine her tears as she begged not only for the safety of her son, but also for the deliverance of her people from the evil pharaoh? Oh, she must have begged the God she served to prove His glory and to spare the life of her precious baby boy. Could she handle anything accept freedom? The bondage was great; the burdens heavy, the chains were thick and tight. She must have pleaded to be set free.

Three months, that is all she dared to keep him in hiding. She opened the basket, placed her child inside, kissed him, I am sure of it, closed the cover. It was time to put the basket into the water, near the reeds.

What water was it? _____

- o   The Nile….the same river that became the final resting place of baby boys that were not spared

- o   The Nile … the river that was crocodile infested

- o   The Nile …where the daughter of Pharaoh bathed

Read verses 4-7 of Exodus 2. There she was, Pharaoh daughter, bathing in the Nile River. What were her servant girls doing?

Pharoah's daughter saw the basket in the reeds, commanded one of the servant girls to get it for her. When she opened the basket, she saw the same beautiful boy. He won her heart. She knew that he was a Hebrew baby. Miriam, who had been watching her brother, appeared and asked if she should find a Hebrew woman to nurse the child.

What happened next? vv 8-10.

Don't you love it? Jochebed was able to nurse her own son, at her own home, and get paid for it? Can you see a Sovereign God at work? How?

When the child was old enough, (some believe when he was around seven years old), Jochebed returned him to Pharaoh's daughter.

What did she name the baby? Why?

Seven Years. Seven informative years in the life of a child. Don't you know Jochebed took advantage of every day to teach her son about God? She must have assumed when he left her home, and moved into the home of the Pharaoh, he would no longer hear about Yahweh. She must have taught him how to pray, how to ask for hope in despair, help in trouble, peace in storms, how to trust in God, how to stand even when afraid, and to not become comfortable with the chains his enemy would attempt to place around him.

Her legacy is remembered in Hebrew 11, the chapter of "Faith Heroes." Read about her, and the son she filled with God, in Hebrews 11:23, 27.

Yes, Jochebed's name rightly means, Yahweh's glory.

Rahab

The book of Joshua is a fascinating book. Before completely understanding the book, however, it is important to know certain facts about the events that took place prior to the beginning of the events in the book of Joshua. The Israelites had wandered for years in the desert, hoping to reach the Promised Land of Canaan, which God had promised to Abraham and his descendants. The Israelites had endured famine, slavery, and then the desert for years. Moses had been their "deliverer" and leader. After Moses death, God appointed Joshua as the one to lead the people to their promised destination. The task would be a great one, but God had already done some amazing things before the people.

As we look at Joshua chapter 2, the preparations were being made to scout the land and prepare to take the city of Jericho.

Read Joshua 2:1-24.

In this passage, Joshua sent out spies. Why?

_____

Jericho was located in the Jordan Valley, north of the Dead Sea. In addition to its significance here, Jericho is a significant city from the New Testament. It was the home of Zacchaeus (Luke 19:1-9), where Jesus healed the blind (Matthew 20:29-34), and along the route where the Good Samaritan assisted the man who was attacked by robbers (Luke 10:30-36).

Where did the spies stay?

_____

What did Rahab do for a living? _____

Rahab was a prostitute, a harlot. Most likely she was an innkeeper who offered her "services" to the men who lodged in her place. Her occupation obviously affected her reputation. She lived an immoral life.

It was not for immoral purposes that the spies stopped at her place; merely it was the place in Jericho for travelers. We discover in the sixth chapter that Jericho is a fortified city that was surrounded by a wall. Rahab's house was a key location. Verse 6 states that it had a roof, and verse 24 gives insight that her house was built into the wall of the city and had a window that was on the outside wall. The flat rooftop was a key feature as it had a view of both inside and outside the city wall. The spies would have been safe there and out of view from the passer-by.

In verses 4-5, who found out that the spies visited Rahab's house?

_____

What was his request?

_____

_____

What was Rahab's response?

_____

_____

_____

She lied. By lying she put herself at risk. Her lie was quite different than most lies. Most lies are told to protect the one telling the lie, or to put someone else at risk. She knew that if the king knew she was hiding the spies, she could have been killed. We will consider her lie shortly, but first let's take a closer look at what was on the roof.

What did she have on her roof? (v 6) _____

Flax is a textile fiber used to make linen. Its stalks are cultivated, split and peeled, then soaked in water, and finally dried in the sun on flat roofs. After this process, the flax could be used to form clothing articles, cords, and bands.

Rahab had her flax drying flat in the sun on her roof; a perfect place for the men to hide. I smile as I remember the countless hours I played hide and seek with my children when they were young. My son, especially was the king at hiding under stuff and camouflaging the surrounding so I would not even look for him in that spot. In a more spiritual thought process, I believe we try to hide from God, under the "flax on our roofs" hoping He won't find us there. But He knows. Have you ever tried to hide from God? When? Why? Maybe you are still hiding. He knows where you are, you know. And He knows what you are doing.

Let's take another brief stop and contemplate how God doesn't waste any detail or event in one's life. Rahab's lifestyle and occupation did not take God by surprise. He knew what she was, where she lived, and what she did. He had a plan, and it involved Rahab, with her faults, mistakes, and background. I love how God crosses all barriers, looks past the chains of shame, and chooses to use the most unlikely candidates to accomplish His will.

What about you? Can you identify a time in your life that God looked past your stain, and used you, restored you, or simply let you know He was there? Record some of the details below.

_____

_____

_____

I, for one, am thankful, God sees all, knows all, and still loves us.

Verses 8-13 shed light on the reason she lied, and what her negotiation would be. I love her little negotiation speech in this passage. Today it might sound like this: "Okay, so here's the scoop. I have hidden you up here because I know who you are, why you are here, and who sent you….this is what I want from you …" So perhaps it was more reverent than that. I clearly watch too much *Law and Order*!

Record below what Rahab told the spies she knew about their God. (vv 9-10)

_____

_____

Look closely at verse 11. Unbelievers are aware of what God has done. They may not know how to express it, but they know He is responsible. They know the power of prayer. It is our responsibility to point them to the works of God, and give God the glory.

Verse 12 she set before them her request. What was it?

_____

_____

She knew what God had done, and what He was going to do next. She was afraid and she longed for her people and her family, to be rescued from the destruction of the city. Their safety and hers was the reason she lied, and put her own life at risk. She must have believed their God cared about her too. She was right.

Read chapter 2:14-21. Did the spies agree? _____

The spies promised her their kindness and faithfulness. I do a little gulp here. Anyone with me? There are times I have a hard time extending my kindness and faithfulness to people whom, in my opinion, may not be "worthy." People let us down. They walk away. They lie. They make costly mistakes. I ride my pious horse, looking with disdain on lifestyles and wrongdoings, until I recall that God's grace extends beyond my reach. NO ONE is beyond the reach of God's grace. No one. Not me. Not you.

What does she use to let the spies down from the window? (Remember the window was on the outside wall? Perfect!)

_____

Yes, a scarlet cord. Most likely one she herself had made from flax. Another amazing detail that God wants us to know. She probably had no idea at the time she was braiding it that it would eventually be an item used for her rescue! The scarlet cord; we will return to this cord shortly!

She gave the spies further instruction for their safety, and they in turn gave her some. What final mandate was given to Rahab?

_____

She tied the scarlet cord to the window. We are going to fast forward now to Joshua chapter 6, passing through the Jordan River, which parted when the priests put their feet in the water. We will also pass over the memorial stones set up as a reminder of the goodness of God. We pick up the story in Joshua 6 when God gave Joshua the orders to march around the city of Jericho six days consecutively. On the seventh day, they were to march six times blowing horns, and on the seventh time around, they were to shout and the walls would collapse.

Read Joshua 6:20-27. It happened just as God had said. Every part of the city was destroyed, as well as everyone in it. Joshua told the spies to go find Rahab. I love what the Word tells us in verse 23. Who did they get and where did they take them?

_____

Verse 25 gives us another detail about Rahab. What is it?

_____

Rahab did not hesitate like Lot's wife did. She left behind everything ... her sin, her life-style, her shame. She willingly and eagerly left the city, and so did her family. The scarlet cord was used to rescue them. It is no coincidence that the cord is scarlet in color. Write Isaiah 1:18 below.

_____

_____

Jesus blood was shed so her sins and ours could be covered and forgiven. Rahab became a believer. Her story is one of courage, redemption, and victory. She married Salmon, and together they became the parents of Boaz and their lineage led all the way to Jesus. (Ruth 4:18-22, Matthew 1:5)

Read Hebrews 11:31. Rahab is included in the great chapter of faith. By faith Rahab… God chose to honor her for her great faith and her great works (James 2:25). Why? I have a few thoughts.

1. Rahab rose above what she had done. It was not about what she was, but who she became.

2. God looked beyond her reputation and her weaknesses and saw her potential.

3. She had faith to believe God could and would save her. He transformed her.

4. She accepted the freedom and the clean start God offered.

Do you know a "Rahab?" Or maybe you can identify with her. Either way, isn't it time to stop believing the junk we hear and believe God instead?

Delilah

Manipulation. We have either been in the grips of manipulation or have used it to get our way. Either way, the effects can be disastrous. The word is defined as a tool used to gain control, cleverly, unfairly, or unscrupulously. Ouch! We will look at how powerful this tool really is, and learn to guard ourselves against it and from using it.

Even though we do not read much about Delilah, actually just this chapter, I find her intriguing, almost haunting. Her character is less than appropriate in moral standings, and yet she finds herself connected to Samson, a man who had been set apart to be a Nazarite (read about his birth in Judges 13). His parents were godly people, but Samson was not. He was a user of women and perhaps even a bit arrogant. His life reflected immorality as well. The story of Samson and Delilah played out like a soap opera. But, ladies, what unforgettable life lessons await us in the study of Judges 16. Read the chapter in its entirety.

In the first three verses of chapter 16, we learn that Samson is a "wanted" man. The Gazites have him surrounded and are waiting for the right moment to get him. We also start to learn details about Delilah. I believe we can agree that Delilah is not the kind of gal we want our daughters to pick as a role model, or our sons to date.

Verse 4 makes me ask: What is wrong with this picture? Do you see it? The Bible says that Samson fell in love with Delilah, but there is no mention of a love that Delilah has for Samson. Doesn't that smell like trouble to you? Sure enough, as we read on, she became a tool that the Philistines used to trap Samson.

What was their arrangement?

_____

_____

_____

That is it. They get the man; she gets the money. Money, too much of it or too little of it, either way, it can be dangerous. Isn't it unbelievable the power money has over mankind?

So, just as planned, she asked Samson why he was so strong, and how he could become helpless. Samson lied to her, repeatedly. Delilah was not happy; how dare he lie to her? It never ceases to amaze me how an individual, who already is in the midst of betrayal of some kind, gets upset when he or she is "mistreated." We see it on television and movies all the time. I know you know what I mean … there is a killer on the loose. The police close in on him. They have him cornered, and the killer throws his hands up in the air, and begs, "don't shoot." What is up with that? Okay, let's move on; back to Delilah.

Samson did finally tell Delilah the truth, and it became his downfall for sure. Let's look closer at how she was able to bring him to that point. Delilah had some clever manipulation maneuvers. Let's look at them.

1. Deception

In verse 6, Delilah started her game. She asked Samson outright. "Where does your strength come from, and how could someone make you helpless?" Samson had no idea of the plot, or the money she would get if she could render him helpless. Apparently no shame or guilt in her deception either.

We can do this can we not? We present things, or we word things to our spouse, children, boss, or whomever, to get the information we really want. Most likely, we are so good at it that our target does not know what we are doing. I believe there are times we do not see it in ourselves. What about you? Have you ever used deception to get what you wanted? If so, describe it below, using discretion of course.

_____

_____

_____

2. Resentment

This blows my mind. Delilah was up to no good. She was trying to trick this man who apparently loved her, and when he didn't level straight with her, she gave it to him! Read verse 10. She told him that he had mocked her! How ironic is that? Who is mocking whom? She told him again in verse 13 and 15. Now think with me. Have you ever used resentment to get your way? Ouch! We do not want to be treated poorly, yet we still want the liberty to treat others that way if it works to our advantage. Again, ouch!

3. Nagging

Now, I know you ladies that read this do not have to watch yourself with this, but I can be a real nag, if I am not careful. Read verse 16. What does it say was happening to Samson, and why?

_____

_____

_____

She nagged day after day, pled with him, and wore him out. Yikes. How many men, or women, feel worn out and the life has been drained from them because someone has nagged them so badly? It is time to ask God to show you if you are a nagger, and if He says, yes, then ask Him to give you the strength to change your ways. There has to be a better way to communicate!

It seems that there are not many positive qualities in this gal, and unfortunately there is one more sad detail in this story. Samson did tell her the truth about his strength. With her eyes still on the money she would receive, she carried out her manipulation with more insult and deception. Reread verse 19. Where was Samson when the Philistines finally got him?

_____

_____

Yes, asleep on her lap. Unbelievable. Even sadder still, read verse 20.

... But he did not know that the Lord had left him.

Wow. Ladies, may it never be said of us that our influence or our manipulation has been so overwhelming that we have been responsible for weakening the spiritual walk of another.

Before we leave Delilah behind, let's decide to put aside corrosive behavior. What have we learned?

- Mocking and demeaning words should have no place in our communication.

- It is time to let go of grudges, bitterness, and unforgiveness in our relationships.

- Nagging is a poor form of communication.

- Showing respect is key to healthy relationships.

- Don't let anyone or anything get between you and God.

- Don't allow yourself to come between someone else and God.

It is time to pray! Ask for God's grace to be who He wants you to be. Make things right if God has prompted you to do so.

Naomí & Ruth

Bitterness and Depression. The Oxford American Dictionary defines bitterness this way: *(of people or their feelings or behavior) angry, hurt, or resentful because of one's bad experiences or a sense of unjust treatment.* It defines depression this way: *severe despondency and dejection typically felt over a period of time and accompanied by feelings of hopelessness and inadequacy.* Whew...that is harsh. But I have discovered that life is harsh. Someone once said that life is 10% what happens to you and 90% how you respond. But exactly what do we do when life and its struggles hit us so hard that we don't know how we are even breathing? Worse yet, as Christians, we know better than to feel the way we do, and that adds to our condition. Life can be brutal, for all of us. Naomi and Ruth were just like us. They experienced bitterness and depression, and yes maybe even hopelessness. These wonderful ladies are terrific models for us to examine. They never denied their feelings, nor did they hold tightly to the "woe is me" attitude.

As the book of Ruth begins, we are told that there has been a famine in the land of Judah. Because of it, Elimelech left his home in Bethlehem, with his family, and journeyed to Moab and settled there. Read Ruth 1:1-2. List Elimelech's family members.

_____   _____

_____

A nice Christian family of four: dad, mom, and two boys.

They escaped the famine and they lived in a pagan land, east of the Dead Sea, named Moab. It is believed that idol worship was big there, and the Moabites were not believers. While there, tragedy struck our friend, Naomi. Read verses 3-5, what happened to this family?

_____

_____

I am sure you mentioned that Elimelech died, about 10 years later the two boys, Mahlon and Chilion, died. Did you mention the two daughters-in-laws? They most likely were idol worshipers and unbelievers. Sometimes even having wonderful in-laws can be stressful, but can you imagine having your children unequally yoked with non-believers, in a foreign land, as a widow? Perhaps, some of you can.

To me one of the saddest verses in the Bible is verse 5.... *and Naomi was left without her two children and without her husband.* This has to be the greatest grief of all. Few things compare to that heart-breaking feeling of being left alone, permanently. It's a void that no one could ever fill. No one except the Lord. Waiting for Him to fill that void can be trying. We are tempted to give up hope.

Read verses 6-7. News from Naomi's homeland reached Moab. The Lord heard the prayers of His people, and the famine ended. Naomi planned to return. Two things in these verses stand out. The wording in the Holman Christian Standard Version for verse 6 is as follows:

   ...because she had heard in Moab that the Lord had paid attention to His people's needs....

God's timetable is not always the same as ours. It could seem like God either isn't paying attention or He hasn't heard. Have you ever wondered if God was really listening to a cry of yours, and a need you have has gone unmet? Some of us choke at the thought of questioning God's provision. Sometimes I think I have had His attention right along, but it has been **me** that has been distracted and not paying attention to God. What are your thoughts right now?

_____

_____

The second thought I get from these two verses is the preparation to go home. Naomi was a stranger in this land of Moab. I am guessing that it never felt like home to her. When the famine ended, she could finally go home, where she belonged. I have always enjoyed living in the places I have lived. My family and I have made great memories together, but every now and then, there is that homesick feeling that cries, "I want to go home." For me, that is a small rural place in Northern New York. Nothing fancy, nothing touristy, nothing that draws attention from outsiders, but it calls my name, and I long to go back. I love to visit and reminisce with my parents. I love to walk around the house, drive the dirt roads, and remember the wonderful days of growing up. I love to go home. When life slaps me around, and the trials get hard, my heart cries to go home. I imagine Naomi's broken heart longed for home. Can you identify?

Finish reading the first chapter. The three ladies set out on the road home. Naomi tried to persuade her daughters-in-law to stay in Moab.

Why? _____

Who stayed in Moab and who left with Naomi?

_____

Verses 16-17 are often read in a wedding ceremony. It is a beautiful expression of love. Many scholars believe that for Ruth, these words were more than just words of endearment extended toward Naomi, but in fact a declaration of her belief in Naomi's God, a profession of faith, so to speak. So the two, Ruth and Naomi, traveled together, to Bethlehem. We know how meaningful this city is to believers. They, of course, did not know that the one they served would be born there many years later. It is in Bethlehem, that hope is restored, love is found, bitterness and depression wiped away.

I love verse 19. The whole town was excited about their arrival (like a homecoming, a reunion, waiting for the kids to finally be home for the holidays, or the prodigals to be home again).

How did Naomi respond to the local women?

_____

Naomi was bitter. She was devastated. She left full, but returned empty. Life had been hard. She charged the Almighty with her pain. Not to disregard her feelings or her pain, I wonder if much of what Naomi endured was more about Ruth than herself. God used Naomi to get Ruth to Bethlehem. God's plan was to use Ruth as a key player in carrying out His plan of salvation.

78

How about you? Are you a willing vessel to be used by God for someone else's good? Even if it means heartache and loss? Explain why or why not?

_____

According to verse 22, what time of year was it when Naomi and Ruth arrived in Bethlehem?

_____

It was the start of the barley harvest. I grew up on a farm. My daddy loved the harvest season. It was the time of year when he could see the results of his hard work. It was what he worked for all year long, the harvest. For Naomi and Ruth, their season of hope was just beginning. Good things are ahead for them.

Read chapter two. Answer these questions.

Who was Boaz?

_____

What work did Ruth find?

_____

What character qualities do you find in Ruth?

_____

_____

I love this story! I love how we learn how God watches over His children. I love the style and grace that is evident in Ruth. I love the kindness and gentleness in Boaz. This would be another great chick-flick!

Look again at verse 12. Where had Ruth found refuge?

Permit me again to talk about the farm! We had a dairy farm, but in my older teen years, my parents also bought a poultry farm. We had somewhere around 100 cows and 10,000 chickens. Before we had the poultry farm, however, mom had about 20 chickens. I was riding my bike one afternoon around the circle dirt driveway; my dog was running behind me. As I neared the hen house, Mortimer, my dog, barked at the chicks that were running in the pen. The mother hen started to cluck loudly, lifted her wings, and all the little chicks ran underneath them for shelter from the dog. Mortimer would not have hurt them, but there was safety under the wings of their mother. This verse always brings that scene back to my mind.

When I am scared, uncertain, frustrated, and in a head-spin...when life gets tough, I like to run to my Father, and feel the safety that only He can provide. Yes, I too find refuge under His wings.

In the middle of Ruth's despair, because she had also suffered great loss (her husband, her father-in-law, and her brother-in-law had died; she moved from her familiar place to travel and lived with Naomi; she was taking care of her mother-in-law, who was bruised from her own life's journey, and she had a new-found faith), she moved on, even though her journey had not been easy.

How about you? Do you know what it is like to plunge ahead, even though you know you do not have the strength? Have you experienced refuge under God's wings? Perhaps you are still waiting for God to come through? Hang on, my friends,

80

help is on the way.

Read chapter three. Briefly describe Naomi's plan for Ruth to woo Boaz.

_____

_____

Look at verse 18. Ruth followed Naomi's instructions, but what else was she told to do?

_____

Wait. I am not a fan of that word. It seems like much of life we spend waiting for something. Are you waiting on God for something specific? Don't give up. Read Habakkuk 2:3, and Ecclesiastes 3:1. What do you learn from these verses?

_____

Finish reading the story by reading chapter four. What a perfect ending to a wonderful story: a wedding, a baby, happily ever after.

Let's glance one more time at verse 14. The family redeemer, or kinsman redeemer...a picture of Jesus ...

Verse 15: Naomi's life had been renewed, sustained, and love was found. She lifted her grandchild and held him. On her lap was a descendant of her Redeemer, our Redeemer.

God turned their sorrow into joy, their despair into deliverance, and their bitterness into delight. He can and will do the same for you. Allow Him to teach you and lead you through your darkest days.

In the space below, write down your thoughts, your worries, and your sadness. God will pay attention to them, and is already working on your deliverance.

Hannah

Disappointment. Disappointment occurs whenever your life seems shattered; your hopes, your dreams, your expectations; and your heart is broken. At times, our disappointment is so heavy; we experience great pain, physical, mental, and emotional. Someone or something else may be the cause of our sorrow. Whoever and whatever the cause, we may lose the desire to move on, and have a difficult time trusting again. We can learn a lot about dealing with disappointment by studying Hannah.

Read 1 Samuel 1:1-18. Identify the people involved. Who was Elkanah?

_____

_____

Who is Hannah? _____

Who is Peninnah? _____

What is the deal with men and more than one wife? I struggle with it. Obviously it was cultural, yet still not pleasing to God. It was a major issue here in this family. What was the tension between the two wives?

_____

_____

Once again in our study together we read about a woman who

is childless.

According to verse three, what did Elkanah do every year?

_____

We met three more people, who are they?

_____

What kind of portions did Elkanah give his wives?

_____

_____

What does the Scripture say was the reason Hannah had not conceived?

_____

Have you ever experienced some kind of loss, or need unmet, because that is the way God wanted it? How did you react to that? What did you learn through that?

_____

_____

_____

Hannah was devastated and disappointed. Perhaps you can identify with her as well. Peninah was always there taunting her. Why? Because she could. It brought Peninah joy apparently to see Hannah hurt. Haven't we all had that too? As if it isn't bad enough that we feel cheated, we also have to deal with the taunts and pities of others. There are so many obstacles to overcome: loneliness, pain, shame, feeling punished, guilt, loss, and the list could go on and on. Do you know how Hannah must have felt?

_____

_____

How did Hannah physically respond to her "rival?"

_____

_____

Look closely at verse 8. Her husband didn't get it!

It is no secret that men and women do not always understand each other. There is a void in our lives that only God can fill. Men were not created to meet every need in a woman's life, and a woman was not created to meet every need in a man's life. Only God can do that. Until we accept that and allow God to work in us, we will be unfulfilled. Yes indeed, a relationship between a husband and a wife is special and rewarding, but only God can fully satisfy.

According to verses 9-11, what did Hannah do?

_____

_____

We will come back to this, but for now, reread verses 12-14. Once again, Hannah was misunderstood. By whom?

_____

What did he accuse her of being? _____

That would have really aggravated me, but Hannah responded beautifully. Now, let's go back to vv 9-11. Hannah did what we all should do when we are hurt, confused, and disappointed. She cried out to the Lord. She pleaded with God. The Bible says she was deeply hurt, and she cried many tears. Wow, that could be me. How about you?

Hannah asked God to do something very specific for her, and we know God did indeed answer her prayer. Notice how honest she was with Him.

     ...take notice of Your servant's _____

     ...remember me and not _____ *me*

Hannah recognized her pain. She did not try to hide it from God. She was honest with her heart and her Creator. Certainly if He created her, He could help her. She also pleaded with God that He would remember her, and not forget her. I like that. It is nice to be remembered, but even better not to be forgotten. Do you understand the difference?

She brought everything to God. Would you be willing to be that honest with God too? Is there some hurt or some pain, or concern that has you bound? Would you bring it to God right now, and trust Him with your life? What is it?

_____

After Eli misunderstood and accused her of being "tipsy," she explained to him about her broken heart. I love this, especially since I am a pastor's wife; I love knowing that my husband cares and will listen and pray for the people God has entrusted into his care. Hannah felt comfortable and safe enough with this man of God, to share with him as well. That is the way it should be in the House of God. It should be a place of shelter and safety. It ought to be a place to find love and acceptance.

I absolutely love what the Bible tells us Hannah did next. Read it in verse 18.

She got up and moved on with life. This step is usually the one that we skip, and when we do, it keeps us disappointed and in despair. We have to move on in order to move on! Hannah cried out to the Lord. She waited for God to work. She worshipped Him. You know what, girls? Even if God denies what we ask of Him, He still knows best, is still in control, and He still has a plan for us. We must learn to trust Him. So, get down our your knees, cry out to God, then get up and move on, knowing He is there.

Eli told Hannah to go in peace. You too, my friend, go in peace.

Bathsheba

Bad decisions. Life is harsh. Some decisions are life changing and their repercussions are difficult to overcome. Bathsheba's story is a sad one. There is much for us to learn from her. Perhaps, to your amazement, you may see some painful similarities in your life. Do not despair. God still loves you.

Generally the picture we paint of Bathsheba is not a nice one. We have seen her as an adulteress and seductress. But let's give her a closer look to determine if that is a fair assessment of her.

Read 2 Samuel 11:1. Answer these questions to get the background in your mind.

What time of year was it?

_____

It was time for war, but did David go with his men?

_____

In 2 Samuel 11:2, we discover that David was on the rooftop of his palace. It is my understanding that from the roof, he could have seen the kingdom below. He discovered Bathsheba. We will come back to her. David's behavior was not an uncommon practice, and his motivation was not necessarily immoral; but he should have been on the battlefield, not at home. That was his first mistake. But let's face it, how many times have we done the same thing? We found ourselves in a sticky situation because we should have been someplace else, and for whatever reason, we find ourselves where we should

88

not be. Can you identify?

Back to Bathsheba. She was in the privacy of her own home. She was not seeking the king's attention, and most likely did not even know he was watching. She was truly beautiful. David obviously thought so too. He lingered too long in her direction because she was a beautiful **wife**. Someone else's wife.

What was David's next action? Read verses 3-5.

_____

_____

David had not crossed the line in asking about her, however he certainly did when he summoned for her, and when he defiled her. And, yes, Bathsheba should have resisted the invitation to the king's palace (although I am not sure she knew what awaited her), and she definitely stayed too long after she got there. It is hard to know how much freedom she had in the king's presence. She could have been trapped. Scripture does not indicate that her intentions were to be unfaithful to her husband. However, David's heart did not appear to be so innocent. The result of their encounter was sinful intimacy, which ended in a pregnancy. In verse 5, Bathsheba sent that news to David.

David went into panic mode. He arrived at a solution that he believed would take care of Bathsheba and one that covered his own sin. What was it? Read verses 6-8.

_____

What went wrong? (verses 9-11)

_____

_____

David developed another plan…he was a desperate man. What was plan B? (verses 12-13) How did it fail?

_____

_____

_____

Read verses 14-25. What was the final plan that did work?

_____

_____

Think with me about the trouble that Bathsheba faced. Her husband was dead. Murdered. She was pregnant with the King's baby. She could have been put to death.

Now, most likely, we have not been in the exact same situation, but can you feel her pain? How you ever slipped into a pit, and wondered, "how in the world did I get here?" or "why did I let this happen to me?" or "if I ever recover from this, someone is going to pay!" Perhaps, you just feel like a victim because you have been. You are in a mess, and you do not have a clue how you can get out of it unscarred. Uh, huh. Been there.

Read the rest of the chapter. She mourned her husband. But she was David's new wife … the king's wife, and a mother of a son, and probably had to compete for David's attention with all of his other wives. How her heart must have hurt.

The last sentence says to me, "Girl, I know you are hurt, and I hurt with you." God saw what happened to Bathsheba, and he called it evil. As women, we have the tendency to listen to all the wrong voices. Satan tells us we're no good. He tells us it is all our fault. He wants us to believe we blew it, and we will never be worthy again. Have you heard him screaming in your ear? He loves to keep us defeated and depressed. Maybe you have blown it. You have made mistakes. Who hasn't? It may not be easy, but you can recover. Listen to the whisper of the One who created you, provided salvation for you, and calls you beautiful. **God knows.**

Read 2 Samuel 12:15-25. What happened to the baby?

_____

How did David react? _____

Bathsheba grieved another loss. God gave her another son. What was his name? _____

Solomon is another study altogether, but God did bless him with great wisdom and he did eventually sit on the throne.

Bathsheba's life experiences were filled with the best of times, and the worst of times. She had highs and she had lows. She experienced great highs and was the victim of evil plans and schemes. God walked with her through it all. She too is one of us. Trust your Maker, even when life is out of your control.

The Widow of Zarepath

"the brook died up…"

God amazes me how He has all things under control. What we see as despair, obstacles, and disasters, He sees as open doors to show His glory. If only we could see things from Heaven's perspective, our attitudes and our "not so good" moments might be less dramatic. Oh that we would trust Him even when we do not understand.

Read 1 Kings 17:1-9. Once again, let's zero in on the setting and the characters. Jot down what we know.

The characters:

Elijah _____

Ahab _____

Elijah announced to Ahab that there would be a famine in the land. What would be lacking?

_____

Where did God direct Elijah to go? Near what river?

_____

A 'wadi' was a river-bed that was filled with water just during the rainy season.

What did God tell Elijah would be provided for him there?

_____

What did the ravens bring and when?

_____

Jot down what you know about the setting:

Zarepath

_____

Sidon

_____

Who will be providing for Elijah there? _____

Already in these verses we have seen God's sovereignty at work. He knows and He has all things under control. This story starts out being all about Elijah, but God has a much bigger plan and purpose. Read 1 Kings 17:10-12.

We are now introduced to the widow at Zarepath. What do we learn about her in these verses?

_____

_____

More than likely, this widow was a heathen. She did not know the God of Elijah, the God of Israel as a believer. But she no doubt, had heard all about Him.

At this point, she knew not that the Lord brought Elijah to her so she would provide for his physical needs. She was very needy herself, in fact she was preparing for her death as well as her son's. It would seem like she believed this would be their very last meal.

Most of us would have thought that this man to be rude and asking for too much when the need was so great. Another view from Heaven ... God had prepared her own heart for this moment.

Read verses 13-16. Elijah spoke to her about her situation.

He told her not to be _____.

What else did he tell her to do?

_____

_____

Did anyone think, "Yah, right. When was the last time you cooked or baked and nothing ran out?" Considering what was happening in the land, everything was running out. Water, gone... food, gone... flour, gone... life, gone...

But Elijah mentioned the God of Israel, and mentioned what He had said. When God speaks, every situation changes. What do you think she might have been thinking?

_____

_____

Did she do as he requested? _____

What happened?

_____

_____

The miracle did not just happen one time, it happened for many days. My guess is, every day was a test of her faith. {Does God really love me this much? Is God doing this for me, only

94

because of Elijah? Could God really take my despair away?}
Have you ever had questions similar to those? When is it most
difficult to trust in God?

_____

_____

_____

Read on to finish the chapter.

The widow was an owner of a home. She had an upper room
in her home. Probably the entrance to the room would have
been on the outside of the house, and the rooftop held a private
quarter in which Elijah stayed.

What happened to her son?

_____

_____

Before Elijah interceded on his behalf, what did she believe
was happening?

_____

Despair once again knocked at her door. Can you identify?
Just when the Lord comes through in one area of desperation,
another one comes along that causes you to question and doubt
the goodness of God? And what about the blame game we
play? What did I do? What sin caused this? On and on it
goes. Yes, a crisis of faith. Have you noticed that the next test
of our faith seems to be a bit harder than the one before?

How did Elijah help the boy?

_____

_____

What did she believed after her son lived again?

_____

Yes, God reached down in love and grabbed her heart and cut through her chains of despair. He had His eye on her the whole time. He brought a man of God out of Israel to a pagan land. She offered him hospitality, and God used him to bring hope to her and her son. God told her over and over "I Love You; You Can Trust Me!" He tells us the same thing.

96

Job's Wife

Job. Just the name suggests suffering, does it not? The poor guy really had some tough circumstances to overcome. His reaction and response to his suffering were in contrast to his wife's. Why? I believe we may discover that as we continue.

Read Job 1:1-3. Job and his wife most likely were living in the days of Abraham, Isaac, and Jacob (Holman Illustrated Pocket Bible Handbook, p113).

Where did they live? _____

Describe Job.

_____

_____

He was a wealthy man. No doubt about it.

Read verses 4-5. Their children had plenty of parties. Verse five suggests that not all of the activities that occurred at the parties were above reproach. What did Job do on their behalf, and why?

_____

Verses 6-12 record a conversation between God and Satan; they were discussing Job. Something disturbs me about Satan. In verse 7, what had Satan been doing?

_____

Roaming around the earth...the picture of this in my mind makes me sick to my stomach. It is like he is stalking us, and waiting for the right moment to attack. What a loser.

What did Satan suggest was the reason Job feared God?

_____

What did God give Satan permission to do with Job?

_____

_____

God trusted Job. Here's a question to ponder. What kind of discussion would Satan and God have about you?

The remaining verses in this chapter described the horrific tragedies that happen to Job and his family. I love verse 22 though. Write it below.

_____

_____

_____

Job did not blame God. How is that different from what we hear today from people, believers and unbelievers?

In Job 2:1-7, another conversation takes place. For what did God grant permission this time?

_____

Now, we are about to meet Mrs. Job. Read verses 8-10. What did Job do in v 8?

What was Job's wife's reaction and suggestion?

_____

_____

What did Job call her? _____

What was his reasoning? _____

_____

Okay, let's recap. Job and his wife lost everything, even their children. One terrible disaster after another, they hardly had time to recuperate, and another catastrophe hit. We, on this side of the pages of Scripture, know about the conversation between God and Satan…neither Job nor his wife knew.

How would our attitudes toward our own suffering be different if we could see things from Heaven's perspective? If we could know how God would turn the evil intent of our enemy into good, would it make a difference?

Job's faith in God remained in tact through his suffering. It was that fact that aggravated his wife. She apparently did not share the same faith as her husband. She, in fact, criticized his faith, and even went as far as encouraging him to consider suicide. At a time when they should have been finding strength and comfort from each other, she separated herself from him, and resorted to blaming God. They shared the same suffering, but did not cope with it in the same way. Job's wife became bitter, and wanted her husband to be bitter as well.

Why is it so easy to let bitterness rule in our heart?

_____

Why is it important to deal with the bitterness, and not allow it to reign supreme?

_____

_____

How can we encourage others to deal with their bitterness appropriately?

_____

_____

Job's sorrow brought him closer to the God he honored. Job's wife's sorrow led her away; but it was her choice to respond in this way. It is our responsibility to guard our hearts and feed our soul. We choose. God offers His help.

Job's wealth was eventually restored and doubled. Yet, we do not read about his wife again in this book. She did not experience freedom from her chains. But we can. It is time to break the chains of bitterness.

Mary, Jesus' Mother

Chosen. The Oxford American dictionary defines chosen this way: **having been selected as the best or most appropriate.** It's a wonderful word. It suggests that someone or something has been specifically picked. Yes, it is wonderful to be wanted. However, how well I can remember, as I am sure you can too, those uncomfortable moments in gym class, everyone in the class standing in a line, waiting to hear their name to go on a team. The "best" kids were always picked first; the chosen. And yet, some were picked first simply because they were the most popular at the time, not necessarily the best choice for the assigned game. But God never makes mistakes. So, when it was time to choose a gal to be the mother of His One and Only Son, Mary was whom He picked. Why? Because she was the best for the assignment. We will look at her closely to see what made her the perfect choice...the favored one!

Mary and her engagement and announcement by the Angel

Read Luke 1:26-56. Read back a few verses. Whose "sixth month" was being referred to in verse 26? _____

Mary was visited by an angel. Which one? _____

Look up at verse 19-20. Gabriel was there too. Who was he talking to in this verse, and what was his message?

_____

_____

Now look back at Daniel 8:16 and Daniel 9:21. The same angel had a special message for Daniel. Gabriel was an angel who had significant messages at significant times.

The study of angels is so very interesting. Men like Billy Graham have excellent resources on angels, and the Biblical view of them. For this study, the angel Gabriel was the angel sent to tell Mary and Joseph about God's plan for them and for salvation.

Now, back to Mary. Tell me about her:

verses 26-27 tell us what kind of gal she is. She is a

_____.

I like that. Apparently, God likes that too. In today's world the pressure is great for a gal to give up her virginity. Pray for the young girls you know. Ask God to make them strong enough to hold this quality close to them and not give it away. Pray for them to know who they are in Christ and to find their value and worth in Him, and to want His absolute best for them. Abstinence will not be a popular choice. Encourage them to stand strong. It is an embarrassing topic to many, but it is a needed conversation.

We also know she was _____

to a man name_____. What else do we know

about Joseph? _____

Gabriel did indeed have a message for Mary. What kind of woman did he call her? _____

Guess how the dictionary defines the word favored? You got it! Chosen.

God knew from the beginning of time, she would be the one. Now the time was right. He found her, and picked her from among the "line."

He said two other things to her. What were they? (verse 28)

_____

_____

Sometimes we do not recognize good news when we hear it. Granted Mary must have been alarmed at the appearance of the angel. It wasn't everyday Gabriel made visits. She most likely was young, early to mid teens. My guess is she was somewhat scared, yet Gabe said, "rejoice." I remember when my daughters were mid teens; I do not think they would have been rejoicing at an angel's visit. I think they would have been frightened.

But then Gabriel told her the Lord was with her. Wow…that's huge! What would your thoughts have been?

_____

_____

_____

Even after the words of comfort, verse 29 suggests that Mary was still troubled, and wondered what all this could mean. I like to think she was humbled, and might be thinking "why me?" or "who am I that I would be called favored one."

Reread the angels' explanation, verses 30-38.

"do not be afraid"

Women have a tendency to be fearful. How nice it is to have a message from Heaven not to be afraid. Is there anything that is making you fearful right now? Write them down.

_____

_____

What does 1 John 4:18 say takes care of fear?

_____ + _____

Now read, Isaiah 41:10. What are the five reasons given for not being afraid?

_____

_____

_____

_____

_____

"you have found favor with God" (approval, preference, kindness)

How about this? How do you feel about God's favor on your life? Do you accept it graciously; do you find it hard to believe? Are you fighting it? What are your thoughts?

104

Remember how much God loves you. The Bible says He loves you with an everlasting love.

"now listen"

How many times have I heard that in my lifetime! How about you? There is nothing quite like having God say, now listen. Can you relate?

Record a time when you know God told you something and said "now listen."

_____

_____

_____

The words that came next to Mary changed life for her forever. In fact, those words change lives still today. The people who were living at this time were looking for the Messiah. They longed for Him to come. I doubt Mary, even in her dreams, ever thought about being the one to make His entrance possible. But the angel told her she would conceive, give birth to a son, and call Him Jesus. He told her of the plans that God had for His Son.

I love Mary's next question. What was it?

_____

_____

We are so good at asking the obvious. But think about it. She was talking to an angel, sent from Heaven, and he told her she would have a baby, etc. How do you question an angel's knowledge??? But, hello? No intimacy here. How could that possibly be?

Gabriel explained how. This was the miracle part of the announcement; the part that makes it all God! He even mentioned an older lady and relative. He knew Mary would need Elisabeth! More about Elisabeth later.

The next statement is one I have claimed and clung to much of my life.

"For nothing is impossible with God."

Even though it was spoken many many years ago, it is as real today as it was then. Mary definitely needed to hear it, and no doubt those words lingered in her mind in the days and years to come. We need to remember them as well. They can be your lifeline. Are you facing anything that seems too hard, or impossible to you?

_____

_____

Take comfort, my friend. Nothing is impossible with God. Give your concerns to Him; trust Him to take care of it; keep believing!

Mary's answer to Gabriel shows wisdom beyond her years. What was her response?

_____

_____

She basically said, "Lord, here I am. Whatever You want of me, I am Yours." What a statement of absolute submission. I doubt she had any idea what lay ahead for her. She would bring birth to the Messiah, the Son of God. Wow, that's a lot of pressure for a young girl. But God trusted her. I am amazed. Have you ever been there?

Record your memory of being completely at the Lord's bidding.

_____

_____

_____

_____

Perhaps, you have nothing to record. Pray that you are willing to be the "Lord's slave."

Mary and Elizabeth

Let's reread Luke 1:39-45. We have reached the point in this account of where Mary's life connects with Elizabeth. They were two different women, but they shared something that pulled down the barrier of age that separated them. Both ladies were pregnant, and were carrying baby boys that have an amazing role to play in God's plan of salvation.

There are several lessons that jump off the page from these verses.

1. The Importance of Mentors

Women were created with a need to have friends and to make connections. We enjoy having people around to share our stories and experiences, and either cry or rejoice with us. We are drawn to those who have similar beliefs and interests, and who will give us balance. Here we see Titus 2:3-5 come to life. In the relationship between Mary and Elizabeth we find key ingredients to look for in a mentor:

(Luke1:6)_____ and _____

She was helpful to Mary, as well as righteous and obedient to God. I am sure the months Mary had to listen and watch Elizabeth profoundly helped this teen girl and young mother.

Now, think about your own life. Do you have a mentor? Or perhaps you are a mentor. If your answer is no, is it possible that the Lord has tugged on your heart, and you know you either need one, or need to be one to someone else?

2. The Power of Private Moments

Have you ever experienced a time when someone said something to you, or did something for you, and it just blew your mind? How about when you prayed for something specific and you knew no one else had prayed that way, and God answered it? How about reading Scripture, and you read something that jumps right off the page with what seems to be a letter from God to you? I call those "me moments." Private moments, designed by God, just for me! I know you have had yours too. Write about one of them.

I believe Mary had many of these, and we will look at them in the study ahead. Obviously, Gabriel's visit was certainly one of those moments. Here is another one:

She walked into the room, and greeted her cousin. Elizabeth responded.

Write down what she said to Mary.

_____

_____

Can you imagine what went through her mind? Watch and listen for the private moments in your own life. They are there, because God loves you and has a plan for you as well. Can you think of any right now? If so, list them in the margin.

3. The Significance of Worship

Have you heard the term, "worship wars?" I cringe when I hear it used. We were created to worship...why would churches and Christians war over worship? Somehow we have come to believe that if everyone doesn't worship "like me," they are wrong. Things like hymns or praise and worship... traditional or contemporary... too loud or not loud enough... standing or sitting... raised hands or hands held close... eyes open or eyes closed... drums or no drums, organ or no organ, freedom or legalism, joy or no joy... and on and on it goes. We forget that we are not created to be cookie cutter believers. We are uniquely and wonderfully made. God created us, knowing how He wants us to worship. God is not confused, believers are. Worship isn't just Sunday mornings; worship is a lifestyle. You can worship through tears and pain.

The book of Psalms describes the many facets of worship. Here, in this passage, Mary is worshipping. Notice what it contains.

- Gratitude (vv 46-49)

- Remembrance and Knowledge of Scripture (vv50-55)

- Humility (v 48)

- Joy (v 47)

When you worship, do so with these same characteristics. God is good, and He has done great things for you. Remember what He has brought you through, recall His faithfulness. Quote scripture back to him. Remember who you are in Him. Come to Him with joy, even if you are hurting.

Now it is time to visit **Matthew's account.**

Read Matthew 1:18-25. This is the way Matthew told the story. He focused more on Joseph, but it is a good thing to study both passages. In verses 18 and 19 we learn of the engagement or betrothal and of the pregnancy of Mary. Joseph knew Mary was pregnant, and he knew about the angel's visit. We are not sure what he thought about what she had told him. The Bible does say he was considering putting her away secretly, not making a public example of her. This, alone, tells us much about the godly character of Joseph. (He too was chosen by God for this purpose.) Let's look at the betrothal of these ancient times.

Betrothal was a formal agreement to marry someone; much like engagement. Within the Jewish culture, the betrothal period was a binding contract. There was to be no physical intimacy, and in order to be released from the contract, a

110

written divorcement had to be issued. The only reason for a broken betrothal would be adultery. An infidelity charge was not only sinful but also unlawful. The punishment could have been performed in public in front of the court of rabbis, or privately in front of witnesses. (See Numbers 5:11-31) The latter was Joseph's mindset. He was a righteous man, and had compassion on Mary.

But again, an angel, sent by God intervened, and spoke to Joseph in a dream. Read verses 20-24. In a perfect world, Joseph would have just believed Mary; however, imagine what the news must have sounded like to him. I am sure Mary was concerned about his reaction, and so grateful that Joseph had an angelic visit too. This just might have been the first bond that drew them together. Did you see the movie *The Nativity*? I loved it! I especially enjoyed watching Mary and Joseph fall in love as they were journeying to Bethlehem.

Mary and the Birth of Jesus

Read Luke 2:1-20.

In the beginning verses, we learn of the census that mandated all from the lineage of David, to return to their hometown to be counted. That meant Joseph traveled to Bethlehem, and of course Mary went with him. What a trip it must have been for her. She was very pregnant! Pregnancies are not the same for all women. Some gals are sick from conception to birth. Some feel better than ever, and still some struggle with the beginning months and gain strength as time goes on. However, when the baby is close to full term, every lady is ready to have her body to herself again. (Yes, sometimes sharing is over-rated!) This trip was long and done on foot and on a donkey. Can you picture it? I traveled to the hospital to deliver my first born in a Chevette, while in the transition stage! My, my ... I could not have handled a donkey, and I do not think my husband would have endured with me until the end. Poor Mary, poor poor Mary .. Okay, poor Joseph.

It was Jesus' birth day ... Mary needed a place to rest and deliver the baby. Joseph looked frantically, but because the town was full of people due to the census, there was no room. Read verse 7.

Record every detail.

_____

_____

_____

_____

Not the typical birth. No delivery room, no doctors, no nurses, no sterile birthing bed, no tests for the baby, no flowers, no blankets ...... simply a feeding trough, cloth, and most likely animals since it was a manger (v 12). Not the birthing room I was able to experience or want, yet there is something nostalgic, something right about the setting. It was how God wanted it, and how He planned it. Amazing. Every year at Christmas time I have longed to visit a farm with a barn full of cows, sheep, and other animals, and sit on hay and read the Christmas story. Maybe one day, I will. Oh how I wonder what Mary's thoughts were. Any ideas?

The rest of our study on Mary, we will visit her in some of the "private moments" of her life, and I want you to record your thoughts. What can you draw from these passages?

Mary and the Shepherds' Visit   Luke 2:15-20

Mary and Simeon   Luke 2:25-35

Mary and Anna   Luke 2:36-38

Mary and the Magi   Matthew 2:1-11

Mary and Jesus at the Temple   Luke 2:41-52

Mary and the Wedding in Cana   John 2:1-11

Mary and the death/Burial/Resurrection   Mark 15:40-44
                                                                              John 19:25-27

Obviously we have not studied every passage with Mary, and this has not been an in-depth study of her, but I hope you have seen her close up in enough events of her life, that you realize you have found a friend. Luke 2:51 characterizes her well. Mary pondered (kept things in her heart). That's it. Some moments are just created for you. God has your name written on them. Cherish them. Hold them close, let them remind you of an awesome God with an awesome love for you.

The Woman At The Well

Thirsty. Dry, parched, arid, gasping, dried-up/out, bone dry, craving, yearning … all of these words are synonyms for the word thirsty according to the Oxford American Dictionary. Have you ever experienced such a thirst that you could say you were bone-dry? I have, both physically and spiritually. I have experienced such a dry spell for God to speak to my heart, that I asked if He even remembered who I was. Funny thing, He missed my fellowship as well. But God wasn't the problem; I was. I have prayed recently, "Lord I love you, but I long to hunger and thirst for more of You." The woman at the well was thirsty for God, yet she did not even recognize the craving within her. As we take a closer look at this woman, may we as she ultimately did, meet the only One who can eliminate our thirst.

The Woman at the Well has a name, obviously, but the Gospel writer chose not to include it in his account of the memorable encounter. Why? I wish I knew; but the lack of her name allows us to identify with her, because in essence, it could be me. It could be you. Oh, perhaps not the same background, or "sin," but certainly the same need for the Savior. As we will see, Jesus broke a lot of "rules" of the ancient times to reach this woman, but He was on a mission, and He found her at a well. Let's get started.

Read John 4:1-42. Verse 4 says He (Jesus) **had** to travel through Samaria. The Greek word for *had* implies *must, necessary, ought, or should.* Why is that so significant? It shows that Jesus was on a mission. There was a need for Him to go through Samaria. The woman at the well was the reason. It was not a popular or normal travel route for a Jew. But,

Jesus, still today, overcomes barriers to meet people where they are. He is sovereign and, no matter how far, how long, or how complicated the trip might be, Jesus will get there.

Let's do a little history lesson! Samaria was located on the road between Judea and Galilee. It registered around 40 miles north of the city of Jerusalem. There was much hostility between the people of Samaria and the people of Judah. Jews, when traveling, often would take another route purposely to avoid travel and communication with the Samaritans. Samaritans were considered by the Jews to be half-breeds, meaning they intermarried with the Gentiles most likely during their captivity by the Assyrians. Knowing this, Jesus crossed social barriers in order to travel through Samaria. He had a God-appointed meeting.

Verses 5-6 identifies the setting. What was the name of the town in Samaria?

_____

At what well does he sit to rest?

_____

What time of day is it? _____

Timing is key here. According to the Roman customs, water was drawn in the early morning or late afternoon. The sixth hour would put Jesus at the well at noon.

Verse 7: A woman of Samaria came to draw water. Perhaps she came at the noon hour to avoid other women who would also be gathering water. Most likely, due to her reputation, she was ridiculed and scorned. I love what Jesus did next. He spoke to her. Not only is the interaction between a Jew and a

115

Samaritan off limits, but men did not speak to women in public. In these ancient times, women were considered inferior to men, and no man would dare speak to a woman with such a bad reputation. So, wow, Jesus not only spoke to her but also asked a favor of her. What was it?

_____

Let's take a short detour from the story, and make an application. Still today, women are not always treated with or viewed with honor. I am not on a feminist kick, but I believe that women are the enemy of the evil one. Satan hates us, and loves to see us abused, misused, and under scrutiny. Isn't it wonderful though, that Jesus continues to cross social barriers, accepts us as we are, and then leads us to the place where He wants us to be.

Have you ever experienced the pain of being mistreated or being scorned by others? If so, how did you cope?

_____

_____

_____

Did you realize that Jesus was for you? He loves you, my friend. Always has, always will.

In verse 9, she questioned Jesus, " Why are you asking me, a Samaritan woman?" She knew the risks He was taking in speaking to her. Have you ever thought, "God, why would you bother with me and my struggles, why would you even bother?" You see, we are not so different after all.

Jesus responded, and I paraphrase, "if you only knew who I am, asking you for water, when I can give you Living Water."

I laugh at her response every time I read it. Again I paraphrase, "Huh? You don't even have a bucket! The well is deep, and how do you expect to get the water from the well? Are you greater than Jacob? It is his well." I can picture myself making a similar response.

This gal did not understand that Jesus was talking in spiritual terms. In the Old Testament, Yahweh (God) was referred to as the Fountain of Living Water (Jeremiah 2:13). He explained it to her in verses 13-14.

He says if we drink from the water He provides we will _____ thirst again.

What kind of life is He taking about?

_____

Verse 15, she says, "sure…that way I won't have to come back here to draw water." Yep, she missed it. What was she thinking about in this answer to Him?

_____

_____

Funny, I like to run from hurt and pain too. Unfortunately I can't always run far enough. There are times I have to stop and deal with it. Can you relate? But, Jesus did not make fun of the Samaritan woman for not understanding, nor did He automatically provide what she asked. Instead He brought the conversation back to where she thought her need might be. Her stronghold, if you will.

Reread verse 16. What does He request next?

_____

_____

What was her response?

_____

_____

Oh, yes, He was well aware that she had had five husbands, and that she was living with a man who was not her husband. He knows everything. I could be wrong, but I have to wonder if the request was to allow her to examine herself. Do you suppose that this gal had been trying to find her worth through being with men? As strange as that may seem, women and girls are desperately attempting to find their worth, their value, their identity, and their purpose in things or people. The hole they are trying to fill can only be filled with Jesus. Letting God provide self worth is necessary. We are who we are because of Him.

Do you know someone who really needs to understand that her value comes from God? Maybe it is you. What could you do to help?

_____

_____

_____

Read again verses 19-24. What does the Samaritan woman say next?

_____

_____

She totally changed the subject. Why did she do that? Perhaps the previous topic came too close to her heart ... it might have been rather convicting, uncomfortable. This time she turned the focus to worship. "Should we worship on our mountain, or in Jerusalem?" (This apparently was an issue between the Jews and Samaritans.)

Again, Jesus answered her question without putting her down. Worship plays a key role in the life of a believer - but worship must be real, in spirit and in truth. Worship is so much more than just music - it's a life-style. It is making everything you do an avenue to give God praise.

In verses 25-26, she spoke of the Messiah. She proclaimed when He comes, He will explain everything. Jesus confessed, "I am He." Can you imagine the gasp she must have voiced?

Some time ago I was given backstage passes to meet Randy Travis before his concert at the New York State Fair. I had been a fan of his for a long time. My daughter and I were in the tent waiting for his arrival. I was nervous, obviously, wondering what in the world would I say to him? When Randy walked into the tent, I gasped and found myself speechless. There he was! In just a few minutes he would shake my hand, and I was thinking I really should say something. What, I was not sure. Now, granted, Randy Travis is not the Messiah, and no it was not like talking to Jesus, but the moment of realization that someone "really big" is next to you is HUGE.

THE Messiah had come through Samaria, stopped at the well for a divine appointment with this Samaritan woman. She needed Him, and she didn't even know it. But He was there for her. Likewise, friends, God meets you too. He is there for you.

When the disciples returned, they were amazed that Jesus was talking to a woman. But they said nothing!   I love what happened next. She left, but what did she leave behind?

_____

What does she tell the men of the town?

_____

_____

I love this!!! She left her water jar. What she thought she needed didn't matter anymore because now she had met Jesus.

Now ladies, let's look deep within our hearts. Many times we come to Jesus with our burdens, our cares, our struggles, and well we should. But most of the time, when we leave Him, we pick all our baggage back up and drag it with us. What this gal did is what we too must do. Leave it all behind. Leave it with Jesus, and allow Him to change us, and give us what we really need. So girls, what is it that you are hanging on to that you need to leave behind? Bitterness? Pain? Suffering? Are you angry with someone? Has someone hurt you or your family? Have you lost something that has you spinning in circles? Can you not breathe; can you not take another step? Give it all to Jesus.

Maybe it would help to write it down. What are you willing to leave at His feet, so you can move on with your life?

_____

_____

_____

She was free. As she left her sin behind her, she was free to share about her encounter with Jesus. She went back to town, not the way she was, but a new creation. She was free. Oh how I love to be free!!

The Bible says because of her words; because she told her story, many in Samaria believed. Tell your story. Be a witness of God's salvation. Many people need to see the Gospel at work in our lives. Pray for opportunities to show and tell about works that only Jesus can do.

The Woman With
An Issue Of Blood

Desperation. The Oxford American Dictionary defines the word this way: hopelessness, despair, distress, anguish, agony, torment, misery, wretchedness, discouragement, and disheartenment. Wow. It is hard to comprehend the emotions involved in those descriptive words, unless you have experienced them. It is unfortunate, but many of us have. Oh, our stories may be different; the causes may be varying, but the affects are very similar. The woman with the issue of blood found in the pages of the Gospels is just like us. Desperate.

We read about the woman with an issue of blood in three of the four Gospels. We will glance at two of them, but look deeply at the account in the book of Mark. Read all three accounts, first, they are listed below, and then check which passage you found most intriguing.

Matthew 9:18-22   _____
Mark 5:21-34   _____
Luke 8:40-48   _____

Jesus had just crossed over to the other side of the Sea of Galilee. As was common, a very large crowd waited by the sea. I LOVE to picture that. I am drawn to the water so many times. It is like it calls my name, and teases me to "come to the water." I believe Jesus loved the water too. Do not misunderstand; I am afraid of the water, I cannot swim. But I love to walk along the shore, wade in a brook, sit on a bench or deck overlooking the water... LOVE IT. God always speaks to me whenever I can get away to the water. How I would have enjoyed walking with Him along the shores of Galilee! In Mark 5, Jesus is at the water's shore.

In Mark's narrative, we see the blending of two lives, two stories, if you will, both of whom are desperate and needy. The first one we meet is a synagogue leader. What is his name? _____

What did he do when he approached Jesus?

_____

What was his request of Jesus?

_____

According to verse 42, how old was his daughter?

_____

Jesus followed Jairus. The huge crowd followed as well and pressed against Him. Ah, the claustrophobic's nightmare!

When I was in college, my sister (who is much shorter and smaller than I) and I went to a concert at the gym/stadium on the college campus. The entryway to the doors (which were locked until "doors open" time) was a sidewalk that was wide at the start and bottlenecked to a narrow entrance at the entry doors. The crowd was large and anxious to get inside, but the doors were locked. People kept coming, and were clearly getting anxious. They pressed against us. When the doors were unlocked, there was such a drive to get inside by the crowd, that my sister was whisked off her feet and literally carried to the door, without anyone holding on to her. It was frightening. Just a few weeks later from that experience, a similar thing happened in Cincinnati, where people were actually killed. A crowd pressing in can be scary. I am not sure what the atmosphere was like in the crowd that was following Jesus, but the Bible says they were pressing against Him. I can picture that.

In verse 25, Mark introduces us to the second desperate person in this story. Who is it?

_____

Read on through verse 26. List her needs.

_____

_____

_____

_____

She was described as a woman in the crowd. Have you ever felt like you were just one in a crowd of many? Not really seen, just there. Perhaps you have longed to be heard or seen, or acknowledged, but nothing. This gal can identify with you!

Twelve years. That's a long time to be hurting, bleeding, and in pain. Her pain was extensive, as it not only included the physical aspect of pain, but the social pain too. This physical burden also made her unclean, and condemned as an outcast.

Now, how about you? Have you ever felt like an outcast? Untouchable...maybe not because of a physical issue like this one; but because of something hidden, or a bad reputation, or a mistake you made earlier in your life. Or it could be because you are a Christian and you take ridicule for that at work, or school, or in the neighborhood.

Yes, 12 years is a long, long time. Or is it? To Jairus it was much too short – he was losing his 12-year-old daughter.

12 years…. 1st grade to 12th grade …that goes by fast.; Disease … 12 years is a long battle. Life is full of perspectives, isn't it?

Do you have an example of a 12-year span, either too short or too long?

_____

_____

_____

Now, let us take a closer look at this sweet woman. She could find no doctor that was able to help her, to make it possible for the bleeding to stop. In fact, she grew worse. Then to add more pain, according to Luke's account, she had lost all of her financial resources. Life for her was hopeless.

Verse 27 (Mark 5) -- She had heard about Jesus. I try to imagine what she must have thought when she heard the crowd gathering around Jesus. I expect she had been praying that He would come. Perhaps, she had seen Him walk by, or maybe she heard the crowd calling His name. Whatever it was that drew her, she made her way through the crowd, through her pain, and managed to get near Jesus. You see, she had had enough. It was time for the bleeding, both physical and emotional, to stop. She knew Jesus was her only Hope left. And there He was! An answer to her prayer!

She touched His robe ... Matthew tells us she touched the tassel on His robe ... maybe just the hem of His garment. What did she say?

She believed Jesus, even just His clothes, would heal her. Do you have that kind of faith? What happened next?

The Bible says instantly the bleeding stopped, and she sensed she was cured of her affliction. Think about that. She **knew** it.

It has been several years since I have gone through some medical issues I had, and the surgery that took care of it. Praise the Lord. What I realized after the recuperation time had passed was that I had felt awful for such a long time, that I forgot what it felt like to be well and feeling good. But when it was over and I had healed, I **knew** it. I had forgotten what it felt like to feel good. I was so familiar with the ugly feeling that it felt normal.

Now, ladies, let me speak in different terms – spiritual terms- do not get comfortable with your pain, bitterness, and anger. It will feel normal, but God has so much more for you. Get to Jesus, only He can restore you.

She knew she was healed, and Jesus knew it too. What was his reaction?

How did the disciples respond?

_____

You've got to love those disciples!!!

Jesus looked around to see who had touched Him. He knew who had. I think He wanted her to know that He knew. He was not okay with just knowing. He looked for her. He wanted to see her face. Don't you love that? When He is there and He makes a situation right, He wants to see us. He looks for us, maybe to let us know He will not let us go on without Him. He is there for us. How we need to drill that in our minds. He loves us.

What happens next is crucial. This newly healed lady stepped out of the crowd. How did she come, what emotions?

_____

She did two things, what were they?

_____

_____

You know what is key here for us to learn? The blessing is in the obedience! What does Jesus call her?

_____

What else did He say?

_____

Look at what He said:

127

"Daughter" He gave her an identity in Him. She was a daughter now - His daughter. God was now her Father. Just moments before her encounter with Him, she was an outcast, now, a family member, with royal blood flowing through her veins, not losing it.

"your faith" He loves it when we trust Him. He desires for us to believe that He is Who He says He is! What I really like about this statement to her is that it suggests that Jesus knew what her heart was thinking. He knew she believed that just a touch of His robe could make her well. Ladies, even when your heart is breaking, and you want to believe, if you act on what your heart longs for, Jesus will recognize your faith.

"has made you well" She was well. Her needs had been met, her shame taken away, and she was no longer unclean. Jesus had healed her.

"go in peace" The word for peace here is shalom, which means *wholeness, full life.* He was telling her she could walk away healed from her affliction. She was free. She was clean.

God is so good. This is such a remarkable story. The woman was healed, and Jairus' daughter, who had died before Jesus got there, was raised to life. So many lessons for us to learn. So many victories to celebrate. The same peace, freedom, and healing that this woman experienced is ours to have, right now, right where you are. What afflictions are you carrying? It could be medical, or it could be emotional, and still it could be spiritual. Do you long for a touch of His garment? You too can "go in peace?" What would stop you? Believe Him. He is trustworthy!

The Woman Caught In Adultery

Forgiven. The *Holman Illustrated Pocket Bible Dictionary* defines forgiveness as a term used to indicate pardon for a fault or excuse; to excuse from payment for a debt owed. It suggests guilt. We have all been there, have we not? Haven't you ever said something awful or untruthful, and it resulted with others hurt or offended? Haven't you ever done something that was sinful and wrong, and it stirred up a mess, and could have, even if it did not get you into trouble? Haven't you ever thought something cruel and hateful, and if people knew what was in your heart, they would be devastated? Absolutely, the intensities of our sins vary, but bottom line, we have all been guilty and deserving of punishment and repercussions. But Jesus' death on the cross, and our acceptance of His salvation provides us with sweet forgiveness. Perhaps the woman caught in adultery heard Jesus say the sweetest words ever said to a sinner, the guilty. They can be your words too.

Sin is ugly. It doesn't matter if it is open sin or hidden sin; it is still ugly. Jesus does not ignore sin, nor does He allow it to continue without consequence, either internal or external. Jesus not only recognizes sin, but He also sees the heart and the motivation behind every word and deed. He extends mercy, grace, and forgiveness, as He deems appropriate. I, for one, am grateful for His love and compassion, as well as His conviction and discipline. I hope you agree.

Read John 8:1-12, and answer some basic questions. (When I was growing up, we lived near the Canadian border at the northern part of New York State. It was before cable and

129

satellite, so the only television stations we could get were Canadian stations. I spent a lot of time with my grandparents, and they watched a show called *W-5*. It was a news and history game show. A guest was behind a curtain. A panel of contestants could ask only 5 kinds of questions, and then had to determine the event the guest represented.) Would you use this format to get the details recorded in this passage?

1. Who?

_____

2. What?

_____

3. Where?

_____

4. When?

_____

5. Why?

_____

The story played out like a courtroom drama, only it was real. It was dawn and Jesus was sitting at the temple complex, teaching the people who had come to Him. The scribes and Pharisees brought a woman caught in adultery and placed her in the center of the gathering. The men demanded her stoning. Jesus rendered a decision.

Let's break it down:

Scribes – Biblical scholars and historians tell us that the scribes were experts in the Law. They were like lawyers in that they were trained to be "gatekeepers" of the law. If a law was broken, they knew it because they had studied and taught

130

the law. They did not extend grace. Jesus was a source of contention with them because He was not "formally" trained as they were. Jesus **is** the authority and He corrected them many times. They hated Him and were closely involved in His death.

Pharisees – The Pharisees were a religious political party during New Testament times. They believed the way to God was through obeying the Law. They were "sticklers" – observing the law was of utmost importance. Yet, they added to the law as it became beneficial to them. They were not in control, but they were controlling.

Do you know any "modern day scribes or Pharisees?" Or perhaps you may be one! Today we might refer to this kind of religious person as legalistic. Legalism is defined as excessive adherence to law.

Read Isaiah 29:13. In *Breaking Free,* Beth Moore describes legalism as one obstacle that blocks our path to freedom and knowing Jesus fully. I recommend the book and/or study. It is a life-changer. God desires for us to enjoy our lives with Him, not endure it with imposed rules, accusations, and expectations. God looks at the heart. We can perform and restrict, but God desires us to obey with our heart, soul, mind, and strength.

Reread verse 6. What was their intent in bringing this woman to Jesus?

Their desire was to trap Jesus, testing His adherence to the Law. They obviously were not concerned about this woman. They were using her to get to Jesus. They cared not about her humiliation or the pain this forced on her. But Jesus knew their evil hearts and their self-righteousness. Jesus also knew this woman. He would right the wrong.

Have you ever been the "fall girl" of someone else's evil plan? I have, and it hurts. The pain lingers what seems like forever. If you know what I am talking about, record your thoughts.

The Crime – Adultery is another ugly word. Before we look at some background, may I say that no sin is unforgiveable? With this particular sin, I find it hard to believe that someone actually plans and hopes for adultery. I think it is one of those sins that an individual can slide into without intending to do so. One thing leads to another, one lie believed, one bad choice, and the snowball effect begins. Then the question remains: "How did I get here? What was I thinking?" Now granted, it is still sin, and there are still devastating consequences for more than just two people. It is still wrong, and because of the world we live in, some do proceed with evil intent. Today's society does not view the seriousness of adultery the same as society did in Bible days.

In Israel's covenant law, adultery was forbidden. (The seventh commandment, *Do not commit adultery.* Exodus 20:14) Read Leviticus 20:10. What was the punishment?

Read Deuteronomy 17:5-6. According to the Mosaic Law, how was this to be determined?

132

This explains the interest the scribes and Pharisees had in the woman they dragged in front of Jesus, but it does not justify the manner and reasoning behind it.

Now, let's look at what happened. When I read verse 3, my heart aches. This poor woman. She was forced in the center of the crowd of people, in front of Jesus. Can you picture her? I see her with her head down in embarrassment, tears streaming down her cheeks, because she knows she could be put to death by stoning, that very moment. There she was, trembling in fear, and guilty of the crime in which she was accused, standing before Jesus, the King of Kings, whether she even knew Him in this way or not. She waited for her sentence, not sure how she was even breathing.

And yet, in front of Jesus is not such a bad place to be, and for her it turned out to be the best place. When things look really bad, where you really need to be, is in front of Jesus so He can meet you there and become all you need.

There is an absence in this scene that bothers me however. Do you see it too? Who was missing?

You got it! The man. He apparently was allowed to go free, even though the law stated that both the man and woman were to be put to death. One more indicator that the scribes and Pharisees were really after Jesus, and this woman was being used for their personal gain. Women had very little value in those days, so she did not matter to them.

Reread verse 6. Can you imagine what this gal was thinking? "Wait, Jesus, what are you doing? You are writing on the ground with your finger. Oh those accusatory fingers!"

I ask again, what about you? Have you felt the discomfort of fingers being pointed at you? Have you heard statements like, 'She did it.' 'It is her.' 'She's the one.' 'Look it's her. Who does she think she is?' 'She's guilty.' Don't those statements make your skin crawl?

But then, what did Jesus do?

He stood up. Oh I like that! He spoke. I like that too! "The one without sin among you should be the first to throw a stone at her." I picture her closing her eyes and waiting for the stones, wondering how long it will take to actually die.

Again, I have to ask. Have you felt like she must have felt? You've been caught, and now you are just waiting for the punishment to come.

Or perhaps, you are the one with the stone. You have been waiting for the moment to pitch the stone at the accused. Finally, justice is here.

Which one are you?

After Jesus spoke, He stooped back down and wrote again in the sand. The lady must have been thinking, "What is happening here?"

Instead of the stones being hurled, what happened?

Who left first? _____

Why do you think the older men left first?

_____

_____

One by one people left. Even that ministers to me. When we go to Jesus with our problems, whatever they may be, one by one, He helps us deal with them, and they leave. One by one they left. The woman, who expected the stones to be thrown at her, heard them drop to the ground...one by one. Her accusers were walking away.

Why? Record why you think the men walked away from the woman.

_____

_____

I do not know what Jesus wrote on the ground. Scripture does not say. We can surmise that what He did write so pierced their hearts, convicting them of their sin, they could only walk away. The older men moved first. Were they hoping the younger ones would follow? Perhaps. Could it be that because of their age, they had witnessed more "life" and experienced more pain, and just didn't have the heart to stay. Perhaps. They probably saw their hearts and their motives like Jesus saw them, and they sadly walked away. What I like best is this:

After the accusers are gone, who is left? _____

When it comes to serious business, when it comes to dealing with sin, when it comes to matters of the heart, it really is just

"Jesus and me", or "Jesus and you." Have you had a time with just you and Jesus? What do you remember most about that encounter?

_____

_____

Think of three words that might describe how the woman might have felt when the men started disappearing.

_____   _____

_____

In verse 10, Jesus spoke directly to the woman, what did He say to her?

_____

_____

When she answered Him, she called Him Lord. She knew Who He was, and what He could do. She knew her need; perhaps what He wrote on the ground was for her as well.

Jesus spoke again to her. Sweet words, what were they?

_____

_____

Jesus addressed a specific need in her life.

Neither do I condemn you. The dictionary defines condemn as expressing complete disapproval of, typically in public; find someone guilty.

Go and sin no more. Jesus released her from her guilt, but also admonished her to stop the sin. She was forgiven. She was free.

Jesus tells us the same thing. Stop it. No more. You're done. Has He ever said those words to you? You see freedom and forgiveness does not open the door for us to be or do whatever we want. It is to stop doing what we shouldn't be doing. Stop whatever it is that has you bound. Precious words…neither do I condemn you. Go and sin no more.

Reread verse 12. Who is the Light of the World?

_____

When we follow Him, we will never walk in _____
but will have the _____ of life.

Step out of the darkness, and into the Light.

The Widow With Two Mites

Needy. Life can surprise us with death, disease, heart-ache, job loss, and the list goes on and on. The key to contentment and dealing with life is the heart. It is what separates the believer from the unbeliever. When our strength is gone, God is there to pick us up and carry us. When we want to be bitter at the journey before us or behind us, only He can soften our hearts and mold them. When we can only look down, He can lift our heads. Yes, we are needy, but in the midst of our need, God can teach us to be generous and to trust Him to meet our every need.

Before we dive into the study of the widow, look back to Mark 11: 27 to discover the setting of this story. Where is Jesus?

_____

Who is there at the temple complex with him, asking questions?

_____

Throughout the eleventh chapter, Jesus was discussing the scribes and the hypocrisy of their lives in contrast to their beliefs. Read Mark 12: 38-40 for Jesus' description of the scribes.

Jesus and the others were sitting in the court of women. This was the part of the temple complex where both men and women gather. However, women could go no farther than this part of the complex. This was also where the treasury, or the offering receptacle was located. Now read Mark 12:41. What was happening while Jesus was speaking?

_____

What did the rich people give?

_____

Read Mark 12:42. Who came next?

_____

What did she give? _____

Why did Jesus say she gave more than anyone?

_____

A mite was the smallest coin and the smallest currency in Palestine. One mite was only worth one-eighth of a cent. One might think her offering was cheap, when in fact, considering what she had; her offering was not only sacrificial but also extravagant.

Widows were vulnerable. In those times, a slave had more position and more money and more ways to earn money than a widow. Unless the widow had family to take care of her needs, she most likely was homeless and poor. Notice the contrasts in this story. First, consider the status of the people.

The widow (v 42):

_____

The other people who brought their offerings (v 43):

_____

Consider the gifts given.

The widow: _____

The other people: _____

Obviously the amount of the offering given by the rich was worth more than the widow's two mites, but which offering did Jesus consider being more valuable?

_____

Why? _____

The Lord recognized her and praised her. Character is much more important to Jesus than wealth, status, or fame. Jesus is more concerned with the attitude of the heart than an actual deed. Let's take a closer look at character. Describe the qualities desired in a believer in these verses.

Philippians 2:3-5

_____

Philippians 2: 13-15

_____

Philippians 4:4-7

_____

Once you have considered the list you have just made, how do you measure up? What are some of your thoughts?

The widow's gift was not enough to meet a specific or a great need, but it was more valuable than any other gift given that

140

day because she gave from her heart. What do these verses tell us about giving?

Acts 20:35

_____

Romans 12:8

_____

What kind of giver are you?

_____

The widow understood that everything she had belonged to God, and she was willing to give it back to Him. What does Psalm 24:1 tells us about ownership?

_____

How does the fact that God owns everything affect you?

_____

_____

Martha

Distractions. As women there are always issues, jobs, expectations, and self-imposed obligations riding on us. These prevent us from concentrating on the things that are more important. Our daily quiet time gets pushed out of our schedules. We find ourselves working and serving at the church, but yet have no time to spend with God. There is something wrong with that picture. Our intentions are fine; our priorities may be off. It is not that serving is wrong, not at all. It may just be misplaced.

Busy, busy, busy. Have you ever felt like there is just not enough of you to go around, nor enough hours in the day to accomplish all that is expected of you, or all that you desire to get done? We definitely live in a jam-packed society. Go, go, go. Do, do, do. Interestingly enough, God says, "Come. Rest. Be Still." Martha was a doer, and I believe she enjoyed her doing. But, like us, she put extra pressure on herself, and could easily allow herself to become distracted by all the "doing" and miss the "being." Do you know what I mean?

Let's take this story one verse at a time. We begin this lesson in the book of Luke chapter 10.

Verse 38   Martha, her sister Mary, and her brother were Jesus' friends. We often saw him visiting with them. According to this verse, whose home was it?

_____

How did Martha receive Jesus?

_____

Do you not love to have company come? I love it. Granted, it can be additional work, but I get such a thrill when I know company is coming. Martha loved to have Jesus visit her too. She welcomed Him. He obviously must have felt at home in this house with His friends.

Do you have friends that you can be yourself with them? No need to worry you will say or do the wrong thing. There is safety with them. They know you and still love you? If you do, write their name(s) down.

_____

Now thank God for them. Those relationships are gifts, and rare.

Verse 39 Here is Mary. We will look at her closer next lesson, but for now, where was she?

_____

What was she doing?

_____

Now I know this is awesome what she was doing. But does it bother anyone other than me that she doesn't seem to be helping? I am thinking, if she would help Martha, then Martha could sit there too! Am I the only one who thinks like that?

Verse 40:   Aha, so now we understand better. How does the Bible describe Martha in this verse?

_____

143

In other words, she was probably doing more than she was required. Busy, busy, busy. She was getting more tired by the minute. I am also thinking that she kept looking at Mary, just sitting there while she was doing all the work. Martha was not only distracted, but now she was mad. So she told Jesus. Remember tattling when you were a child? Same kind of thing.

Finish the statements Martha says to Jesus. (I am using the Holman Christian Standard version.)

Lord, don't you _____?

Have you ever felt that way? Does Jesus care? Does He care that your child is ill? Does He care that your husband is cruel? Does Jesus care that you lost your job? Does He care that you hate your job? Does He care that you are not happy? Does Jesus care that you are lonely? Does He care that you are homeless? Does Jesus care that you are so very sorry? Does He care that you can't go back and make things right? Does Jesus care? Maybe I missed your question. If it helps, complete it yourself.

Does Jesus care that_____?

Read 1 Peter 5:7. What does it say about you?

_____

One of the hardest things to do is to place our cares and our burdens at His feet and leave them there and walk away free from them. Hard, but not impossible.

Back to Martha. What else did she say?

...my sister has left me to serve _____

When we are weary, overworked, and distracted, we can take the self-pity route. No one is helping me. I am all alone. No one knows what I am going through. No one understands. Poor me. Now, before you get too upset with me, let me assure you that these statements are true of all of us, at one time or another. We women do have to do a lot of things on our own. Yes, we are alone. And yes, no one does completely understand. However, if you choose to take this road, please make sure you have not self-inflicted these wounds. It is easy to do. Martha wanted Mary's help....maybe she wanted Mary to offer to help without asking. We do not know the dynamics of their relationship. But as hard as it is for me to admit it, because I like Martha, I think she was whining here, what do you think?

Next statement, So _____ her to give me a hand.

Whoa, what? This seems a little disrespectful to me. How about to you? Perhaps, they had this close of a friendship that Martha was comfortable saying this order to Jesus. Makes me nervous. I wonder if she stomped her foot. We can let ourselves get to this point too if we are not careful. We "blow up" instead of contemplating.

Verse 41   The Lord answered her. "Martha, Martha" Did your parents ever use your name twice? Was it accompanied with a head nod, and a disappointing look? Jesus spoke to her softly.

What did He tell her in this verse?

_____

_____

Worried and upset about many things. Again, it was Martha's perception about the situation. Jesus knew it, but He knew her heart too. Just like He knows yours. So what about it? Are you worried and upset about many things? Want to list them?

Things that worry me (your mind dwells on these troubles or difficulties)

_____

_____

_____

Things that upset me (makes me agitated and flustered)

_____

_____

_____

Read Philippians 4:6. Ecclesiastes 7:9   What do these verses suggest we do?

_____

_____

_____

Verse 42:   Jesus was still talking to Martha. Three more statements, what are they?

_____ thing is _____.

_____ has made the _____
choice.

It will not be _____ away from
her.

Most problems can be solved by realizing one thing…Jesus is all we need. Jesus told Martha that Mary had made the right choice. Two things here:

1. Jesus was not saying that Martha's service was wrong. It was her venting and her judgmental attitude that caused her rebuke.

2. The choices we make are crucial, for every decision. Write down your thoughts on statement #1.

_____

_____

Write down your thoughts on statement #2.

_____

_____

The final words of rebuke to Martha put things into the proper perspective. He basically said, "No." He wasn't going to make Mary help Martha. He said no. I smile. Has God ever told you no? He has me. I have even heard these: Are you kidding? No way. Forget it. Get over it. Move on. Never.

147

One might think that Jesus was scolding Martha; instead He was using the moment she had created, by her own choices, to teach her. Mary was taught at Jesus' feet; Martha was taught on her feet. She had other lessons to learn.

Let's look now at another passage where Martha is present.

Read John 11:1- 16. Answer the following questions about the story.

Who was Lazarus?

_____

What had happened to him?

_____

To whom did Mary and Martha send word to about their brother? _____

What was Jesus response?

_____

According to verse 14-15, what was Jesus' desire?

_____

Read verses 17-27. How long had Lazarus been in the tomb before Jesus arrived?

_____

Once Lazarus' sisters heard that Jesus was coming, what was the response of

Mary?

_____

Martha?

We will return to verses 20-27.

Read verses 28-37. Where did Mary go after Martha returned from being with Jesus?

Where did the Jews go and why?

What did Mary say to Jesus?

What did Jesus do in verse 35? Why?

Finish reading this story, verses 38-44. What did Jesus ask them to do?

What was Martha's response?

Jesus spoke again to Martha; we will come back.

What did Jesus request of Lazarus?

What did He request next?

Now, let's go back and look specifically at Martha in this passage.

What do we know about Martha?

1. Jesus loved her. v. 5

2. She and her sister were mourning their brother's death. v. 19

3. She went to Jesus as soon as she knew He was close by. v. 20

4. In her grief and despair she acknowledged her hurt and belief in Jesus. vv. 21-22

5. She knew the teaching of the Resurrection. v. 24

6. She heard Jesus call Himself the Resurrection and the Life. v. 25

7. She believed. v. 27

8. She said what she was thinking. v. 39

9. She continued to serve. John 12:1-2

Our spiritual walk needs to be in balance. Take the time to sit at His feet and worship, and when the time is right, work and serve Him.

Mary

Sitting At Jesus Feet. Mary loved to be at His feet. She loved Him, and longed to be near Him, learning all she could learn. She was faithful and loyal. Once again, worship is a lifestyle; it is what we were created to do. Mary's life exemplified her desire to worship her Lord.

Revisit Luke 10:38-42.

Mary's response to Jesus in the house was quite different from her sister Martha's. What did Mary do?

_____

What does "sitting at Jesus feet" look like today?

_____

_____

What did Jesus state about Mary's actions?

_____

Yes, Mary made the right choice. She was focused on Him, hungering for His words and guidance. When is your time to regularly focus on Him and His Word?

_____

Do you have a special place that you meet?

_____

Do you remember Mary's reaction to her brother's death? If you need to, reread John 11:20. Martha ran to Jesus as He was on His way to Lazarus. What did Mary do?

_____

John 11:28 Who did Jesus specifically request to see?

_____

John 11:29-32 What did Mary do?

_____

What was her position when she got to Jesus?

_____

What did she tell Him?

_____

Notice it is the same thing that Martha had said to Him in verse 21. They actually were not that different after all!

Let's move on now to John 12:1-8. Once again, we see Martha serving. She had prepared a dinner for the disciples and Jesus. What Mary does next is worth studying.

Recap: Mary takes a _____

and anoints Jesus' _____ and

wipes them dry with her _____.

The house was filled with the _____.

Judas was upset. Why?

_____

What was Jesus' response?

_____

Mary was demonstrating her deep love for Jesus. She worshipped Him with her sacrificial offering to Him.

The Fragrant Oil:

- The jar of perfume was worth more than a year's wages.

- This aromatic ointment was also used to embalm bodies.

Anointing:

- Usually performed on one's head (see Matthew 26:7)

- Usually performed for healing, setting apart, or embalming

- Usually olive oil is used

At one's feet

- Only the lowliest servants would clean feet, which would be dirty and dusty

- An act of humility and submission

Hair

- Typically worn bounded or braided, especially in public

Symbolic

- Preparing His body for burial

- Act of worship

What can we learn from Mary of Bethany?

Mary Magdalene

Freedom. Most of the time, we do not realize the pain of being in bondage until we are set free. We only know we are bound, and a slave to something. Freedom is available through Jesus, His healing, His Word, and our obedience to Him. We all know hurtful experiences. Yet, we do not need to be hindered by them, nor crippled by them. Jesus can set us free. Praise His Name!

What do we know about Mary Magdalene? Read the following passages and discover some biographical information. Luke 8:1-3

Where was she from?

_____

Magdala was a small village on the northwestern side of the Sea of Galilee. Magdalene is not her last name, but rather an indication of where she dwelled. Studies show that it was a place where immorality was rampant.

What was her affliction?

_____

So what are demons? Matthew 25:41

Demons are fallen angels who have joined Satan in his rebellion. Jesus' power and authority cause the demons to submit to His command. Exactly what was it like to be demon-possessed?

Matthew 9:33

Matthew 8:28

Matthew 12:22

Mark 1:26

Luke 9:39

Mary had seven demons. The Bible is not specific with their descriptions. They were cast out of her. Jesus did that. He released her from the grip of the demons, and set her free from their influence over her. Modern day addictions would be similar in nature. As you are aware, the causes of addictions are various (dependence, habits, substances, things, or activities). Name some:

Read Isaiah 61:1-3   What was Jesus sent to do?

_____

_____

_____

The other passages with the mention of Mary are:

Matthew 27:56-61; 28:1

Mark 15:40-47; 16:9

John 19:25; 20:10-18

All of these are centered on Jesus' trial, persecution, and His death.   Mary had become a true follower of Jesus.   She followed and ministered to Him at her own expense.   When others fled when Jesus was arrested, she lingered close to Him. Look at the John 20:10-18 passage.

Where was Mary standing?

_____

She was crying, and she bent to look at something, what?

_____

What did she see?

_____

What did they ask her?

_____

What was her response?

_____

_____

Who did she see when she turned around?

_____

Did she know Him?

_____

Why wouldn't she have known Him? Write down your answer.

_____

_____

She spoke to Him but who did she think He was?

_____

Jesus called her by name. Whew, I love that! She knew then who He was. Don't you love to hear someone call you by your name? I do.

What did she say to Him next?

_____

What did she do next?

_____

_____

"I have seen the Lord." Jesus released her from her bondage. She was grateful, yes, but it went beyond gratefulness. He set her free. She was shouting her victory and His. Her life was changed. Ours can be too. Write your thoughts.

_____

_____

_____

Made in United States
North Haven, CT
06 June 2022

19912354R00088